INPUT PROCESSING AND GRAMMAR INSTRUCTION IN SECOND LANGUAGE ACQUISITION

INPUT PROCESSING AND GRAMMAR INSTRUCTION IN SECOND LANGUAGE ACQUISITION

Bill VanPatten
The University of Illinois at Urbana-Champaign

ABLEX PUBLISHING CORPORATION
NORWOOD, NEW JERSEY

SECOND LANGUAGE LEARNING SERIES
A Monograph Series Dedicated to Studies in Acquisition and Principled Language Instruction

Robert J. Di Pietro, editor

The Catalan Immersion Program: A European Point of View
  Josep Maria Artigal

A Developmental Psycholinguistic Approach to Second Language Teaching
  Traute Taeschner

Reading Development in a Second Language: Theoretical, Empirical, and Classroom Perspectives
  Elizabeth B. Bernhardt

Vygotskian Approaches to Second Language Research
  James P. Lantolf and Gabriela Appel, editors

Bilingualism and Testing: A Special Case of Bias
  Guadalupe Valdes and Richard Figueroa

Elizabeth B. Bernhardt, editor

Input Processing and Grammar Instruction in Second Language Acquisition
  Bill VanPatten

In preparation:
Listen to the Silences: Mexican American Interaction in the Composition Classroom and Community
  Kay Losey

Printed in the United States of America

Library of Congress Cataloging-in-Publication Data

VanPatten, Bill.
   Input processing and grammar instruction in second language
acquisition / Bill VanPatten.
       p.   cm. — (Second language learning)
   ISBN 1–56750–237–7. — ISBN 1–56750–238–5 (pbk.)
   1. Language and languages—Study and teaching. 2. Second language
acquisition. I. Title. II. Series.
P53.V364 1996
418'.007--dc20

                                    96–3502
                                       CIP

Ablex Publishing Corporation
355 Chestnut Street
Norwood, NJ 07648

P

In order to keep this title in print and available to the academic community, this edition
was produced using digital reprint technology in a relatively short print run. This would
not have been attainable using traditional methods. Although the cover has been changed
from its original appearance, the text remains the same and all materials and methods
used still conform to the highest book-making standards.

DEDICATION

To Jim, with love and gratitude for the last 15 years and for encouraging me to spend time in Santa Fe to work on this book.

To Lucy and Ginger (arf-arf, woof-woof-woof, arf, woof-woof, pant, pant, pant) and to Murphy (meow).

TABLE OF CONTENTS

SERIES EDITOR'S PREFACE

Second Language Learning was established by Robert J. Di Pietro in 1987. At that time, he described the series in the following way:

> *Second Language Learning* is intended for the publication of research into second language acquisition and instruction. The series is distinguished from others that address similar topics by two major features. First of all, the volumes in the series are focused in their orientation. They may be authored by one or more persons, but in all cases, their findings come from theoretically coherent and unified research projects. Secondly, they are motivated by the drive to uncover principles of acquisition and instruction rather than by a wish to fulfill some immediate classroom need.

From 1987 until the time of his death, Professor Di Pietro sought out manuscripts that exemplified that description. I am proud to say that he included my work among his selections.

In 1993, I was challenged to try to fill the void left by the untimely death of Bob Di Pietro. That challenge meant carrying on the important work he had begun with the series and finding manuscripts that I believed Bob himself would have chosen. I am convinced that Bob would have included Bill VanPatten's book, *Input Processing and Grammar Instruction in Second Language Acquisition,* for sure. *Input Processing and Grammar Instruction in Second Language Acquisition* indeed focuses on the specific issue of grammar and its role in contemporary language instruction. Rather than providing us with a picture of grammar as yet another skill area, the VanPatten book helps us to see that grammar is the cognitive glue that holds the second language comprehension and use process together. This book provides data generated on extensive in-class work and places those data against the backdrop of the research literature in second language acquisition. *Input Processing and Grammar Instruction in Second Language Acquisition* is the first contribution to the series *Second Language Learning* under my editorship. I am confident that readers will find it to be an outstanding contribution to the research literature in applied linguistics.

—**Elizabeth B. Bernhardt**
Series Editor

PREFACE

The intent of this book is to review a model of second language input processing and examine one particular approach to grammar instruction derived from it—namely, processing instruction, an input-based focus on form that stands in direct contrast to more traditional forms of foreign language grammar instruction involving output practice (drill, question-answer, and so on). This book also aims to summarize the research on processing instruction and to address potential challenges to and questions about both the model on which it is based and the instruction itself.

Of particular importance, I would like to think, is that a research agenda on both input processing and processing instruction has emerged. Whether or not one buys into processing instruction and the claims made in this book, my most minimal hope is that students of classroom language acquisition take note of the research agenda. For example, in Chapter 4, the reader should focus not only on the research itself, but also on how the research has evolved, what questions arise from each study that are subsequently addressed by additional research, and how the various studies build on each other to form a cohesive body of empirical investigation. The student of classroom language acquisition should also note that there is more research to be done and that this is not only a natural part of research-based language teaching but a desirable one as well. Far too often, in my opinion, claims are made about language teaching (or language learning, for that matter) with too little empirical evidence to back them up. We have learned too much and come too far since the demise of habit formation theory and audio-lingual methodology to accept the latest thing to come down the pike without asking for some evidence.

This book arises from 10 years of thinking about and reflecting on second language acquisition and the role of input in the development of a grammatical system. I am indebted to a number of colleagues and graduate students who have listened to me or read my work. These colleagues and students have asked me to clarify issues or have challenged me on various aspects of both input processing and processing instruction. It has been a stimulating decade for me. I hope that I have correctly remembered all of you for the following list (alphabetically arranged, by the way)—and don't worry; no one will hold you responsible for any of the ideas, good or not-so-good, in this book.

Rodney Bransdorfer	James F. Lee
Teresa Cadierno	Patsy Lightbown
An Chung Cheng	Barry McLaughlin
Rick de Graaf	Diane Musumeci
Donna Deans Binkowski	Soile Oikkenon
Rod Ellis	Isabel Pereira
William R. Glass	Cristina Sanz
Jan Hulstijn	Richard W. Schmidt
Peter Jordens	Bonnie Schwartz
Stephen Krashen	Tracy David Terrell (in memoriam)
	Helmut Zobl

My thanks also go to the Research Board of the University of Illinois for its constant support of much of my empirical research since I arrived in 1985 and to the university for the sabbatical leave for the fall semester 1994 during which I drafted this book. My thanks also go to Ivan Schulman for his support during his tenure as head of the department. It is not easy being an applied linguist in a department largely dedicated to literary and cultural studies, but Ivan has always had a unique vision about where language departments should be headed. I hope he is enjoying his retirement. I would also like to thank the following colleagues who have supported me when the chips were down. You are the greatest: Evelyn Garfield, Antonino Musumeci, Sandy Savignon, Linde Brocato, Elena Delgado, Susan Gonzo, Numa Markee.

Another round of thanks goes to my students from the 1995 spring semester graduate seminar who read the manuscript of this book and provided feedback that helped to make the content more accessible: Louise Neary, Pedro Córdova, Joe Barcroft, Renato Rodríguez, Nuria Sagarra, Karin Millard, María José González, Marisol Fernández.

A special thanks goes to Elizabeth Bernhardt (series editor), the anonymous reviewers of the manuscript of this book, and to Anne Trowbridge plus all the folks from Ablex Publishing for making this book a reality. Your efforts are very much appreciated.

My final thanks go to James F. Lee. His name appears on the dedication page, but of all people to whom I owe gratitude to him I owe the most. I wish everyone could have the support, encouragement, absolute confidence, and love of someone special that I do. Life can be fragile, and I don't want to miss any opportunities to say, "I love you."

—Bill VanPatten
Champaign, Illinois
February 19, 1996
(my birthday...)

chapter **1**

INTRODUCTION

Some might argue that second language acquisition is an independent nonapplied discipline (Gass & Schachter, 1989, p. 4), that its goal is to explain how second languages are learned. More particularly, the goal of second language acquisition research is to understand how a linguistic system develops in a learner's head. Like any number of theoretical domains, a researcher in second language acquisition identifies a phenomenon, examines the variables involved, conducts research (or theorizes about the phenomenon), and eventually draws a conclusion about the phenomenon. In this view, second language acquisition is divorced of pedagogical interests. This is not to say that issues in second language teaching are not important; instead, pedagogy must reflect an understanding of (a) theory of second language acquisition and pedagogical principles and practices should be firmly grounded in theory and research.

Others would argue that second language acquisition research is only as important as the pedagogical issues that motivate it. In this view, what should be researched are those matters that directly affect teachers and learners in classrooms; research and theorizing should be at the service of pedagogy and not divorced from it.

The present book is one attempt to link second language acquisition theory and research with pedagogical issues. Its focus is grammar instruction. Although other books have been written about grammar instruction from a variety of theoretical viewpoints (e.g., Ellis, 1990; Odlin, 1994; Rutherford, 1987), this book aims to describe a particular approach to grammar instruction called processing instruction. The book also aims to motivate this approach via theory and to offer research to support it. In so doing, we hope to show that second language acquisition theory and research can make some very direct—and hopefully welcomed—suggestions for second language teaching.

WHAT IS PROCESSING INSTRUCTION?

Processing instruction is a type of grammar instruction whose purpose is to affect the ways in which learners attend to input data. It is input-based, as opposed to output-based, is consonant with both general second language acquisition theory and communicative language teaching. It was first described in VanPatten (1991) and has since been described, discussed and researched in a number of publications (Cadierno, 1992, 1995; Cheng, 1995; Lee & VanPatten, 1995; VanPatten, 1993; VanPatten & Cadierno, 1993; VanPatten & Oikkenon, 1996; VanPatten & Sanz, 1995). Since we will describe processing instruction in detail in Chapter 3, we will not go into its specific characteristics nor the specifics of the theory that underlies it in this introductory chapter. Instead we will begin by asking what the motivation for processing instruction is. After all, grammar instruction has been around for a long time. For centuries learners have received explanations about how the second language works, followed by practice using grammar rules and paradigms. Why question this approach to grammar instruction?

MOTIVATION FOR PROCESSING INSTRUCTION

Traditional Approaches to Grammar Instruction

Over the centuries, grammar instruction has taken a variety of forms depending on the overall goal of instruction. Under grammar-translation approaches, the goal of foreign language learning was to learn a language in order to read texts (i.e., the great works of literature) in that language. As Richards and Rodgers (1986) describe it,

> [grammar translation] approaches the language first through detailed analysis of its grammar rules, followed by application of this knowledge to the task of translating sentences and texts into and out of the target language. It hence views language learning as consisting of little more than memorizing rules and facts in order to understand and manipulate the morphology and syntax of the foreign language (p. 3).

Although certain scholar-educators challenged the grammar-translation approach in the nineteenth and early twentieth centuries in an effort to place emphasis on the acquisition of oral language skills (e.g., F. Gouin and the famous "Gouin series," the Direct Method), grammar-translation was a dominant language teaching paradigm well into the middle part of the twentieth century. A major revolution in language teaching did not occur until the advent of audiolingual methodology. Born of the army's interest in developing oral language skills during World War II, audiolingual methodology was supported by American structural linguistics and the theory of behaviorism. Explicit grammar instruction was eschewed under this methodology. Instead, the grammatical system of the language was to be "uncovered" by the learner through rote practice of sentence patterns, memorization of dialogues, and other "oral practice." Under audiolingual methodology, the grammatical system was viewed as a set of habits to be internalized through consistent practice and reinforcement. It was not necessary for learners to know what rules they were learning, but it was necessary for them to correctly repeat, transform, and perform other manipulations on sentences orally as a necessary first step toward communicative ability with the language.

As behaviorism and linguistic structuralism lost favor in the sixties, cognitive code learning began to emerge. Essentially an evolution of audiolingualism, cognitive code theory said that for learning to happen, learners must know what they are learning and have some conscious mental representation of it before practicing. Those who advanced a cognitive-code approach to classroom language learning advocated that grammar explanation and examples should proceed sentence manipulation. By the 1970s, most classrooms in the United States involved some version or other of audiolingualism or cognitive-code theory.

Interestingly, not much was actually known about the processes and products of second language acquisition before 1970. Seen as the intersection of psychology and linguistics, second language acquisition was thought to be not much different from more general learning in which knowledge and practice were seen to go hand-in-hand. Syntactic rules, verbal and nominal paradigms, and other descriptions of linguistic features of the second language constituted the knowledge that learners needed to internalize. Sentence drills involving manipulations, transformations, and the like, were the diet of classroom practice. To "internalize" language meant to memorize and regurgitate linguistic forms. Savignon (1983) summarizes the tenets underlying the language program she taught in before she developed her ideas on communicative competence and the language classroom. The fifth tenet is perhaps the best description of what was happening in classrooms by someone who was an instructor at the time:

> The basic unit of practice should always be a complete structure. Production should precede from repetition to substitution and continue until responses are automatic. Spontaneous expression should be delayed until the more advanced levels of instruction. Production errors in structural or phonological features mean that the patterns have not received sufficient prior drilling (p. 20).

By the late 1960s and early 1970s, a particular approach to grammar learning via practice was codified by Paulston (1972). She described a taxonomy of practice types and advocated a sequential ordering of them. In this taxonomy, Paulston claimed that mechanical practice should precede meaningful practice. Meaningful practice should in turn precede communicative practice for any given linguistic structure or grammatical feature. This sequencing as well as characteristics of each practice type are displayed in Figure 1-1. At the time of the writing of this book, this sequential ordering of practice types and an emphasis on oral production was still the staple of most second language textbooks published in the United States, something that we will review in Chapter 3.

The Role of Input

Since 1970, we have gained many insights into second language acquisition, owing to an ever increasing number of researchers with special interest in the field. Although we are far from completely understanding how second language acquisition happens, some aspects of second language acquisition are clear to the research community. One such aspect involves the role of input and the acquisition of grammar. To illustrate, we will examine quotations from a number of well-known researchers.

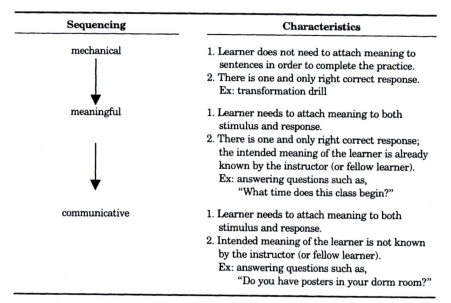

Sequencing	Characteristics
mechanical	1. Learner does not need to attach meaning to sentences in order to complete the practice. 2. There is one and only right correct response. Ex: transformation drill
meaningful	1. Learner needs to attach meaning to both stimulus and response. 2. There is one and only right correct response; the intended meaning of the learner is already known by the instructor (or fellow learner). Ex: answering questions such as, "What time does this class begin?"
communicative	1. Learner needs to attach meaning to both stimulus and response. 2. Intended meaning of the learner is not known by the instructor (or fellow learner). Ex: answering questions such as, "Do you have posters in your dorm room?"

Figure 1-1.   Paulston's taxonomy of practice types and their sequential ordering.

The Input Hypothesis claims that humans acquire language in only one way—by understanding messages, or by receiving "comprehensible input" (Krashen, 1985, p. 2).

All cases of successful first and second language acquisition are characterized by the availability of comprehensible input. (Larsen-Freeman & Long, 1991, p. 142).

It is self-evident that L2 acquisition can only take place when the learner has access to input in the L2. This input may come in written or spoken form. In the case of spoken input, it may occur in the context of interaction (i.e., the learner's attempts to converse with a native speaker, a teacher, or another learner) or in the context of non-reciprocal discourse (for example, listening to the radio or watching a film) (Ellis, 1994, p. 26).

For the knowledge system of a particular language to grow, the acquirer must have exposure to instances or exemplars of that particular language. Without such exposure language development will not take place (Schwartz, 1993, p. 148).

The L2 learner's task bears a strong resemblance to that of the L1 learner. L2 learners are also faced with the problem of making sense of input data, of coming up with a system which will account for that data, and whcih will allow them to understand and produce structures of the L2. Thus, their task can be conceived of as follows, equivalent to the L1 acquisition task (White, 1989, p. 37).

Although the above cited researchers hold different perspectives on second language acquisition and may use different frameworks with which they investigate factors affecting second language acquisition, all concur in that meaning-bearing input is essential to second language acquisition. What this means is that learners must be exposed to samples of language (and in great amounts) that are used to communicate information. Some researchers also suggest that the input must be modified or adjusted during the course of interaction (e.g., Long, 1983) or be comprehensible to the learner. Whether modified or not, without meaning-bearing input learners cannot build a mental representation of the grammar that must eventually underlie their use of language. This role of input is depicted in Figure 1-2. The term "developing system" refers to the mental representation of the second language the learner is constructing over time. It is this recognition of the essential role of input in second language acquisition that leads one to rethink traditional approaches to grammar instruction. The obvious question is whether traditional grammar instruction is consonant with the idea that input is the basic building block for the construction of a mental repre-

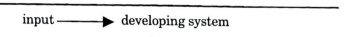

Figure 1-2.   A simplistic view of the role of input and aquisition.

sentation of the second language grammar.

Recall that traditional grammar instruction involves explanation and subsequent oral practice. This approach presumably results in a mental representation of the grammar that will underlie communicative performance. However, if meaning-bearing input is one of the essential building blocks of acquisition, where is the meaning-bearing input in *output* practice? With its emphasis on output practice, a traditional approach to grammar instruction ignores the crucial role of input in second language acquisition—and the definition of input in second language acquisition does not include instructors' explanations about how the second language works. The definition of input is limited to meaning-bearing input, language that the learner hears or sees that is used to communicate a message. Thus, in traditional instruction, learners practice a form or structure, but they are not getting the input that is needed to construct the mental representation of the structure itself. This is analogous to attempting to manipulate the exhaust fumes (output) of a car to make it run better. If we want to improve the performance of a car, we might first want to look into using a better grade of gasoline (input).

In contrast to a traditional approach to grammar instruction, processing instruction is an input-based approach to focus on form. Appropriate processing instruction activities, as described in detail in Chapter 3, do not ask the learner to produce targeted grammatical items; instead, learners are pushed to attend to properties of the language *during activities in which they hear or see language that expresses some meaning.* These activities contain "structured input"—purposefully manipulated sentences and discourse that carry meaning. During these activities, the learner is pushed to attend to particular features of language while listening or reading. Thus, attention to features in input becomes an integral part of the grammar acquisition process. Unlike traditional instruction then, Processing instruction is consistent with the input-based nature of acquisition.

Input Processing and Intake

To be sure, processing instruction was not born solely out of the acknowledged role of input in second language acquisition. If input were all that were needed for successful language acquisition, then there may be no need for a focus on form at all; natural, free occurring input should do the trick! This is not the case, however. Some, if not many learners, evidence lack of acquisition or only partial acquisition of the grammar of a language even with exposure to input. Although we can suggest that this is due to a conspiracy of factors (Sharwood Smith, 1985) involving sociolinguistic, attitudinal, motivational, contextual, cognitive, and other factors known to affect second language acquisition, our focus in this book is a psycholinguistic one. From a purely psycholinguistic perspective, we note that what language learners hear and see may not be what gets processed. Input does not simply enter the brain as the learner is exposed to it. If this were true, then acquisition would be almost instantaneous. What is clear is that learners filter input; they possess internal processors that act on the input and only part of the input makes its way into the developing system at any given time. The part of input that learners process is generally called intake, a term first coined by Corder (1967). What learners do to input during comprehension—that is, how intake is derived—is called input processing (see Figure 1-3). Although not the focus of this book, those processes involved in the incorporation of intake into the developing system are referred to as accommodation and restructuring. We will touch upon these processes briefly in Chapter 5 as we examine the relationship between input processing and accommodation–restructuring *vis à vis* Universal Grammar and first language transfer. A third set of processes, those that are used by learners to access the developing system to create output, are not represented in the figure at this time.

Recognizing that learners process input and that intake is ultimately the data made available to the developing system raises a number of questions: What is the nature of input processing? What strategies or mechanisms are involved? Could input processing be responsible in some way for the partial or incomplete nature of the developing system? Chapter 2 of this book takes up the first two questions, and it is the answer to the third question that has more directly motivated processing instruction. Given that acquisition is intake-dependent and that intake is in turn input-dependent, it is clear that input processing must play some role in the formation and development of the learner's linguistic system. From the perspective of a focus on form, then, we can ask the following question: Can input processing be manipu-

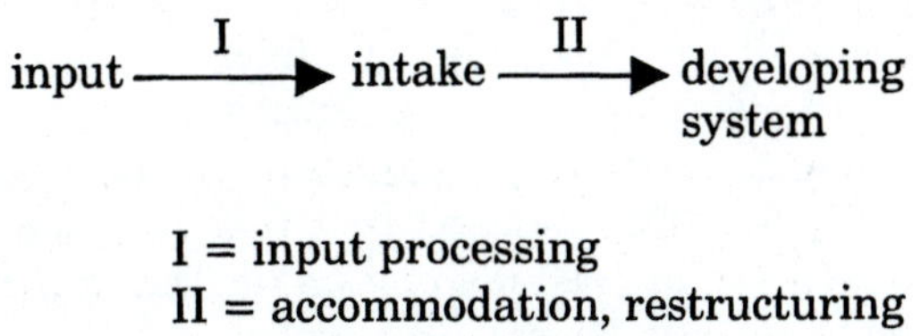

input $\xrightarrow{\text{I}}$ intake $\xrightarrow{\text{II}}$ developing system

I = input processing
II = accommodation, restructuring

Figure 1-3.   Two sets of processes in second language acquisition.

lated, altered, or enhanced in order to make intake grammatically richer? It is this particular question that has led directly to the development of processing instruction. As we will see in Chapter 3, processing instruction does not mean that just any old input activity is viable and that learners will subsequently make the correct targeted form-meaning connections. Processing instruction always considers the nature of input processing and attempts to alter learners' default processing strategies if they do not work to create optimum intake. Processing instruction thus is beneficial when it identifies an incorrect or less than optimal processing strategy and then fashions input activities that help to circumvent the strategy.

To sum up, processing instruction is an input-based, psycholinguistically motivated approach to focus on form. Unlike traditional instruction with an emphasis on rule learning and rule application during output activities, the purpose of processing instruction is to alter how learners process input and to encourage better form-meaning mapping that results in grammatically richer intake. This in turn should have a positive effect on the nature of the developing system.

THE ORGANIZATION OF THIS BOOK

The remainder of this book is dedicated to exploring processing instruction in detail. In Chapter 2 we will examine the nature of input processing. Relying on experimental and descriptive evidence, we will outline a set of processes learners use to make form-meaning connections during input processing. Framed as processing principles, we will see how these processes result in filtered input data and how they help to explain the partial and sometimes incorrect nature of the grammatical system evolving in the learner's head.

In Chapter 3 we will examine processing instruction in some detail reviewing a set of guidelines for developing what have come to be called structured input activities. We will look closely at the types of activities that learners are engaged in and how they are derived from the insights about input processing described in Chapter 2.

In Chapter 4 we will review empirical research on the effects of processing instruction. Although processing instruction is a relatively new idea, a number of studies have been conducted that point to its benefits. This research examines the effects of processing instruction using a variety of linguistic features: syntactic, morphological and inflectional, and lexico-semantic. The findings of these studies suggest that processing instruction is an attractive alternative to traditional instruction for focusing on form in the communicative and input-rich language classroom.

In Chapter 5 we explore a number of potential criticisms of both input processing and processing instruction. Specifically we will examine the relationship between input processing and Universal Grammar (UG) as we explore some issues in the acquisition of syntax. We will also see why input processing and processing instruction do not succumb to the criticisms leveled at cognitive approaches to second language acquisition and teaching. In this chapter, we see that an important research agenda in the acquisition and teaching of syntax emerge.

THE INTENDED AUDIENCE FOR THIS BOOK

This book is intended for scholars and nonbeginning students of second language acquisition and teaching. Although we have attempted to limit the use of jargon and to explain relevant terms and concepts as we proceed, we might not be able to completely satisfy the needs of beginning students of second language acquisition in this regard. As is the case with many books and research reports on specialized topics in second language acquisition, the reader will most likely benefit from introductory readings on second language acquisition before reading the present book. Nonetheless, the majority of concepts should be accessible to most readers including the beginning student of second language acquisition.

TERMS USED IN THIS BOOK

A number of terms are frequently used in this book. Since researchers may use these terms differentially and because readers may impart a meaning to a particular term because of their own backgrounds, these terms are defined in the following. When used in the remainder of this book, these terms will imply the indicated meanings.

Developing system refers to the complex of mental representations that as an aggregate constitutes the learner's underlying knowledge of the second language (phonology, syntax, morphology, etc.). Some researchers refer to this as the "learner's grammar," the learner's "interlanguage," or the learner's "(linguistic) competence" (see, e.g., Schwartz, 1993; Selinker, 1972).

Explicit instruction refers to planned and organized teaching designed to inform learners of how the second language works. Explicit instruction generally involves some kind of explanation (explicit information about the language) and some kind of practice, but not always. What makes explicit instruction explicit is the information provided to the learner about how the language works.

Focus on form refers to any manner in which the learner's attention is somehow drawn to the formal properties of the second language and how they work. This can happen in or out of a classroom. However, the attention drawn to form happens within a communicative context so that clarification requestions (e.g., "Do you mean _____?") and other interactional devices may serve to draw a learners attention to formal elements during the expression of meaning. (see Long, 1991).

Form (also called *grammatical form*) refers to surface features of language that include verbal and nominal morphology (i.e., inflections) and functional items such as prepositions, articles, pronouns, and other "non-content" words.

Form-meaning mapping (also called *form-meaning connection*) refers to the connection that the learner's internal processors make between referential real-world meaning and how that meaning is encoded linguistically. An example is the form-meaning connection between the inflectional suffix /-t/ and "past time reference" in English. Form-meaning mappings happen during input processing and are necessary for the building of mental representations (see below).

Input is used to mean comprehensible, meaning-bearing input. This is restricted to samples of second language that learners hear or see to which they attend for its propositional content (message). This term is synonymous with Krashen's use of input and Schwartz's used of PLD (primary linguistic data). It does *not* refer to explanations about the second language nor explicitly formulated information given to learners about grammatical properties of the second language (see Krashen, 1982; Schwartz, 1993).

Input processing refers to the derivation of intake from input during comprehension.

Intake is the subset of filtered input that serves as the data for accommodation by the developing system. It is the input that has been processed in some way by the learner during the act of comprehension. Intake is *not* synonymous with internalized language. Instead, intake are the data made available for further processing (e.g., internalization) once the input has been processed.

Mental representation refers to the largely unconscious representation of any aspect of the linguistic system in the learner's head. This representation may or may not exist as a rule, paradigm, and so on, since the psychological validity of rules and paradigms is debated by linguists and psycholinguists (see, e.g., Bybee, 1991).

Processing strategy refers to the (largely) unconscious strategies that learners use to map meaning onto input sentences such as assigning agency to a noun in a sentence or determining plurality versus non-plurality of a noun. These strategies are psycholinguistic in nature and are *not* synonymous with the concept of "learning strategies" frequently discussed in the literature; these latter being deliberate attempts to control one's learning (e.g., using nemonic devices to remember words).

Syntax refers to the structural properties of sentences and the rules that constrain the shape that sentences may take. This contrasts with *grammar*, which encompasses syntax (cf. developing system) (see Chomsky, 1988; White, 1989).

chapter **2**

INPUT PROCESSING IN
SECOND LANGUAGE ACQUISITION

INTRODUCTION

As seen in Chapter 1, there is a consensus among second language researchers that input is an essential component of second language acquisition. Learners use input in order to construct a mental representation of the grammar that they are acquiring. However, there is also consensus that not all of input is attended to. Learners filter the input, processing it so that only a reduced subset of the input—called intake—is made available for accommodation by the developing system. What do learners attend to in the input, and why? What strategies direct how learners' make form-meaning connections? What does intake, as opposed to the input look like?

Since input is a critical aspect of second language acquisition, the reader may think that there would be a plethora of studies describing input processing. Unfortunately, this is not the case. Most empirical studies on input treat issues such as linguistic properties of input and modification of input (see, e.g., Ellis, 1994 [Chapter 7]; the collection in Gass & Madden, 1985; Larsen-Freeman & Long, 1991 [Chapter 5]). Input processing only recently has become the focus of research in second language circles and actual empirical studies are few. Nonetheless, there is enough research, both theoretical and empirical, to begin developing a model of input processing. The point of the present chapter is to summarize that research and develop a set of processing principles that form the nucleus of a model of how learners derive intake from input. These principles can, in turn, serve as points of departure for further research.

The chapter is divided into three major sections. The first deals with cognitive aspects of input processing. In this section we will draw upon various constructs from cognitive psychology, most notably *attention*, and argue that second language learners are limited capacity processors. As such, they can only attend to so much linguistic data at a time in the input during on-line comprehension. We will see that a cognitive approach to understanding input processing yields important insights into the acquisition of morphology, in particular, nominal and verbal inflections. We will see also that a cognitive approach offers insights into the acquisition of functional categories such as articles and prepositions.

The second major section deals with sentence-level aspects of input processing. Here we are concerned with how learners assign grammatical (subject and object) and semantic (agent and patient) roles to nouns. Our focus will be on what is called the "first noun strategy." We will suggest that in the acquisition of a variable word order language like Spanish, this particular processing strategy may have a substantial effect on the developing system. It is this particular strategy that informed the first published study on processing instruction (VanPatten & Cadierno, 1993).

The third major section focuses on a number of issues related to input processing generated by the discussion in the first two sections. Here we examine consciousness and awareness, language transfer, and other models related to input processing, mostly from first language studies. Our point here will be to show that the principles and model of second language input processing developed in this chapter are congruent with other aspects of second language theories. We will show also that related models of language processing are complementary but not inclusive of the ideas presented in this chapter.

ATTENTION AND INPUT PROCESSING

The Principles

Our aim in this section will be to motivate and offer evidence for the following principles in second language input processing. P1 and P2 represent two major principles with P1(a)–(c) representing corollaries to P1.

P1. Learners process input for meaning before they process it for form.
    P1(a). Learners process content words in the input before anything else.
    P1(b). Learners prefer processing lexical items to grammatical items (e.g., morphological markings) for semantic information.
    P1(c). Learners prefer processing "more meaningful" morphology before "less" or "nonmeaningful morphology."

P2. For learners to process form that is not meaningful, they must be able to process informational or communicative content at no (or little) cost to attention.

In order to understand the motivation for these principles, we must first examine the cognitive psychology construct of attention

Attention

As I write at this moment, there are a number of stimuli that threaten to overwhelm me. There is the constant humming of the laser printer, the steady rush of cars on the street, the faint sound of the TV coming from the other room, birds chirping, the clicking of the keyboard, and the sound of neighbors next door. And these are just the auditory stimuli. Although all stimuli are perceived (that is, the *sounds* are perceived initially), we rarely run into any kind of cognitive overload. Instead we function quite well because our brains are equipped with processors that selectively attend to incoming data. Selective attention occurs because orientation of attention brings particular stimuli into focal attention rather than allowing them to be merely perceived (Lachman, Lachman, & Butterfield, 1979). As an example, when writing I orient my attention to the computer screen, which subsequently helps to filter out other competing (visual) stimuli.

Attention is an important construct for learning. Researchers in cognition generally believe that learning takes place via attention. People simply don't learn unless they are attending to the stimulus to be learned. In first language acquisition, for instance, Slobin has argued that the degree to which linguistic information is acquired is determined by whether or not the information is attended to.

> ...the only linguistic material that can figure in language-making are stretches of speech that *attract the child's attention to a sufficient degree to be noticed and held in memory* (Slobin, 1985, p. 1164, emphasis added).

The belief that children learn their mother tongue as well as second languages effortlessly is folklore at best: Children must attend to incoming data if they are to eventually incorporate them into a linguistic system (See Peters, 1985, for further discussion of the effortful nature of L1 acquisition.)

From the perspective of second-language acquisition, Schmidt has provided the profession with an excellent synthesis and analysis of the literature on attention, consciousness, and learning. Arguing against any kind of subconscious or subliminal learning, Schmidt concludes that as far as input processing in second language acquisition is concerned, adult language learning requires attention to form in the input. (See also his more recent discussion in Schmidt, 1994.)

> The existing data are compatible with a very strong hypothesis: *You can't learn a foreign language (or anything else, for that matter) through subliminal perception* (Schmidt, 1990, p. 142, emphasis added).

However, attention is effortful, and cognitive psychologists generally agree that attention involves a limited capacity to deal with stimuli: Only so much incoming data can be attended to at a given time. This is particularly true of competing stimuli that engage the same modality, for example, the aural modality (Wickens, 1984). Although it is the case that most people can walk and chew gum at the same time, it is not the case that most people can watch TV, listen to the radio, talk on the phone, and attend to all the aural linguistic data of each activity at the same time. As a human cognitive activity, language comprehension consumes a great deal of attentional resources, a notion that will become important when we discuss the push for learners to get meaning from the input. As Just and Carpenter (1993) describe it, comprehension involves computations in working memory. Although a number of these computations can proceed simultaneously (at least during native speaker comprehension of the first language), Just and Carpenter note that

> if the number of processes [during on-line comprehension] is large or, more precisely, if the amount of activiation they try to propagate would exceed the capacity, then their attempts at propagation are scaled back to a level that keeps the total activation within the maximum bound.... When the task demands exceed the available resources, then both storage and computational functions [within working memory] are degregraded (p. 4).

One of the processes (or computations) that is carried out during attention is *detection*. Detection is the "process that selects, or engages, a particular and specific bit of information" (Tomlin and Villa, 1994, p. 192). It is the process by which data are registered in working memory and is what makes a particular stimulus or piece of data available for further processing, that is, for accommodation in the case of acquisition. It is not enough, then, that learners simply attend to data; particular data must be detected if learning is to occur. In this way, detection is a subprocess of attention and is the aspect of input processing most directly related to the derivation of intake.

Two features of detection are relevant for the present discussion.

1. Detected information causes great interference with the processing of other information.
2. Detected information exhausts more attentional resources than even orientation of attention (Tomlin and Villa, 1994, p. 192).

What the preceding discussion suggests is that even if, say, a speech stream is attended to by a second language learner, the internal processors may not detect all of the linguistic data. Detecting one bit of information (piece of linguistic data) may interfere with the detection of others by consuming available resources in working memory. The central issue for second language acquisition research is how learners' internal processors allocate attentional resources during on-line processing. In short, what causes certain (linguistic) stimuli in the input to be detected and not others? (Note: from here on *processing* will be a cover term used for attending to and detecting linguistic data in the input.)

The Push to Get Meaning

It is important to recall that input refers to meaning-bearing input. This is language that the learner hears that encodes a message. The communicative goal of the learner is to comprehend the message, to understand what the speaker said. (Although input may be written, we will focus here on aural input.) For this reason, we posit P1.

P1. Learners process input for meaning before they process it for form.

Simply put, P1 states that learners are driven to look for the message in the input ("What is this person saying to me?") before looking for how that message is encoded. The principle is consistent with the observations of other researchers in both first language acquisition and second language acquisition (e.g., Faerch and Kasper, 1986; Klein, 1986; Peters, 1985; Sharwood Smith, 1986; Swain and Lapkin, 1989; Wong-Fillmore, 1976). In first language acquisition, for example, Peters (1985) lists a number of Operating Principles that guide children in processing input. Her first principle, however, is a general one regarding the push to get meaning.

> EX: MEANING: Pay attention to utterances that have a readily identifiable meaning. Extract and remember sound sequences that have a clear connection to a clear context. (p. 1034)

What this means is that first language acquisition is part of the act of comprehension. Learners are constantly seeking some way to map *what* they understand with *how* they heard it.

In second language acquisition, Sharwood Smith (1986) states a similar position when he distinguishes between processing for communication and processing for acquisition. He says that

> It is therefore appropriate to speak of linguistic input as having dual relevance.

At moment X, the learner's main aim may be to extract meaning and survive or succeed in a given interchange of messages. In this case, only those aspects of the input which will aid the learner in this communicative endeavor (linguistic or otherwise) will be relevant in this first sense: *the learner will interpret for meaning* (p. 243, emphasis original).

Although meaning and form are not necessarily mutually exclusive, a point taken up later in this chapter, P1 would lead us to conclude that form and meaning may compete for processing resources. In other words, when all else is equal, form and meaning compete for detection—with meaning generally winning out. Form here is defined as surface features of language: verbal inflections, nominal inflections, particles, functors, and so forth. (We will take up abstract syntactic rules in Chapter 5.) Again, our point of departure is that comprehension is effortful for second language learners and consumes a great deal of on-line attentional resources.

That learners process input for meaning before they process it for form leads us to ask *what* in the input learners would attend to in order to get meaning. A logical place to begin would be with content words. All second language learners come to the task of acquisition knowing what content words are. Intuitively they know that these words are the building blocks of meaning and the initial stages of language acquisition have been characterized in many reports mainly as vocabulary getting. If comprehension is effortful for beginning and intermediate learners, it seems logical, then, that their attentional resources will be directed toward the detection of content words to help them grasp the meaning of an utterance (see also Sharwood Smith, 1986, pp. 245–260). We thus posit P1(a) as a subprinciple to P1.

P1(a). Learners process content words in the input before anything else.

P1(a) receives support in both first language and second language research by the fact that learners in input-rich environments tend to pick out and start using single words or whole unanalyzed chunks of language (which they treat as content words) in the early stages and then combine these to form utterances. In child first language acquisition the early one- and two-word stages of acquisition are well-documented, with children producing utterances like those produced by Peter, a two-year-old, in the following interchange:

Peter: (finding a car) Get more.
Lois: You're gonna put more wheels on the dump truck?
Peter: Dump truck. Wheels. Dump truck. (Lightbown and Spada, 1993, p. 3).

One could argue that Peter's and other children's production of one- and two-word utterances as well as unanalyzed chunks is the result of speech processing constraints and not input processing constraints. However, at some point, output also must offer some indication of what has gotten processed in the input (in addition to how it was stored), a point argued by Peters (1983, 1985). Her data on child first language acquisition convincingly show the child focusing on isolated words and unanalyzed chunks of language in the input, extracting these, and subsequently using them in his own speech. The child might process incorrectly, as the example that follows demonstrates, but it is clear that the child somehow is attempting to isolate content words and connect these to meaning.

> Adult: That's an elephant, isn't it?
>   What is it?
> Adam: Init. (Peters, 1985, p. 1035)

Radford (1990), working within a generative approach, argues pretty much the same point. He notes that the intial stages of first language acquisition involve developing an elementary vocabulary that is acategorical (without grammar or grammatical properties) in nature. Children pass through a pre-linguistic stage (e.g., babbling without words) and a one-word stage before they start to put words together and show evidence of having cateogorized them into nouns, verbs, and so on, or having assigned grammatical categories to them such as subject and object (see Radford, 1990, Chapter 2).

The primacy of content words in processing input is evidenced in second language acquisition as well. Again, early stage learners create output by stringing together content words and unanalyzed chunks: *Why test?, no drink beer, me gusta las clases,* are typical sentences for early stage learners. As in first language acquisition, this stage of output is suggestive of how the input has been processed. But P1(a) receives support from several experimental studies as well. Klein (1986, Chapter 5) reports on research conducted on adult second language acquirers of German living in Germany. Using a sentence repetition task, he asked language learners to repeat stimulus sentences immediately upon hearing them. He found an overwhelming tendency for subjects to pick out and repeat content words, with the more advanced learners being the only subjects able to pick out and repeat grammatical items such as auxiliary verbs and articles.

Mangubhai (1991) also found evidence for a primacy of lexical items in input processing. In his study, he gave five adults lessons in Hindi using Total Physical Response over a period of 10 weeks. He periodically examined what he called "their processing behaviours," in our terms, their processing strategies. He found that all learners focused on lexical words to a greater or lesser degree in order to get meaning from the TPR input. Mangubhai shows that one learner, Barry, was absolutely consistent in this regard as he "reduced the load on his working memory by stripping the input to content words (cf., Shapira, 1978)" (Mangubhai, 1991, p. 283).

Additional experimental evidence comes from VanPatten (1990). In this experiment different levels of subjects listened to a short passage on inflation in their second language, Spanish. After listening, subjects were asked immediately to perform free written recalls in English, their first language. They were instructed to write down anything and everything they could remember. These recall protocols subsequently were scored for the number of correct idea units recalled, using Carrell's (1985) definition of idea unit:

> Each unit consists of a single clause (main or subordinate, including adverbial and relative clauses). Each infinitival construction, gerundive, nominalized verb phrase, and conjunct [is also] a separate idea unit. In addition, optional and/or heavy prepositional phrases [are also] idea units (p. 737).

As part of the experimental design, subjects were assigned to one of four groups: (1) listen to the passage only; (2) listen to the passage and note any

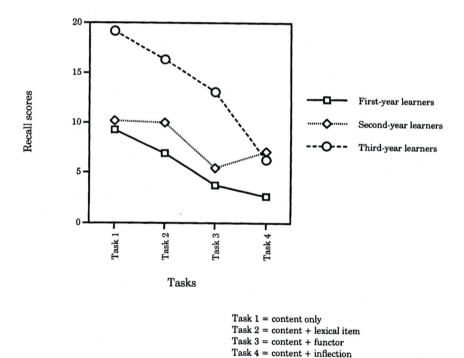

Task 1 = content only
Task 2 = content + lexical item
Task 3 = content + functor
Task 4 = content + inflection

FIGURE 2-1. Recall scores by task and level of learners (based on VanPatten, 1990).

and all occurrences of the content word *inflación*; (3) listen to the passage and note any and all occurrences of the definite article *la*; (4) listen to the passage and note any and all occurrences of the verbal inflection *-n*. "Noting" was operationalized by having subjects place a check mark, slash, or any other kind of mark on a blank sheet of paper each time they noted the target item. It should be pointed out that the passage was constructed so that the content word, the definite article and the verbal inflection occurred 11 times each and were evenly distributed throughout the passage. P1(a) would predict that if comprehension is effortful for learners (uses up attentional resources) and if learners are processing content words in the input before anything else, then those subjects in group (2) should perform better than those in groups (3) and (4). The results bore this out. Subjects in the passage plus content word group recalled as many idea units as those in the passage only group. Subjects in groups (3) and (4) who were asked to attend to a grammatical feature in addition to the overall content of the passage, recalled significantly fewer idea units compared with groups (1) and (2). Indeed, the scores for groups (3) and (4) dropped dramatically, as illustrated in Figure 2-1. That the explicit processing of the content lexical item did not interfere with comprehension is congruent with the idea that content lexical items are of primary importance during second language input processing (at least in the early stages of acquisition).

Meaning and Form: Lexical and Grammatical Encoding

P1(a) has consequences in terms of which surface grammatical features get processed and which do not. A great number of grammatical features encode some kind of semantic information. For example, the verbal inflection *-ó* in Spanish encodes PAST as in *habló*, "he spoke." The English verbal inflection *-s* encodes third person singular. The plural inflection *-i* on nouns in Italian signals more than one as in *ragazzi*, "boys" (cf., *ragazzo*, "boy"). However, what is equally true is that many of these same semantic notions are expressed lexically in a language. In addition to being encoded in *-ó*, pastness is a semantic notion also conveyed by the words *ayer*, "yesterday," *el año pasado*, "last year," and *hace un mes*, "a month ago" in Spanish. Third person is a semantic notion underlying not only *-s* in English but also the nouns "María," "cat," and "he." Also, plurality is not only encoded in the *-i* of *ragazzi*, but also in words such as *due*, "two" and *molti*, "many." Given that learners are initially driven to process content words before anything else, we thus arrive at the following principle.

P1(b). Learners prefer processing lexical items to grammatical items (e.g., morphology) for semantic information.

This principle suggests, then, that learners first attend to and detect lexical markers of plurality before grammatical markers of plurality, that they attend to and detect lexical markers of temporal reference before verbal inflections of tense, and so on.

There are two different kinds of evidence in the second language literature to support P1(b). The first are those data that report how tense is first encoded in learner output. Typically, learners mark time early in the acquisition of verb morphology through lexical items (e.g., *yesterday, last week*) and only subsequently begin to add past-tense verb markings to their linguistic repertoire (Bardovi-Harlig, 1992). This appears to be the pattern for both classroom and nonclassroom learners. Again, if one assumes that output is partially (if not mostly) shaped by the intake derived from input, then these data are consistent with the principle that lexical items are more likely to be attended to than verb morphology if both mark the same semantic feature. (It is worth noting that similar evidence exists for the acquisition of plurality with learners initially marking plurality lexically, e.g., *two dog, many problem*. The same is true with third person singular, e.g., *she go, he sleep*. For some discussion, see Pica, 1985, as well as the literature on pidgins and creoles, e.g., Todd, 1974.)

Recent empirical research provides evidence for P1(b) by specifically focusing on tense. Cadierno, Glass, VanPatten, and Lee (1991) report on the effect of providing classroom learners of Spanish as a second language with two different kinds of discourse level input, that is, a listening passage: one in which temporal adverbials are present and one in which they are absent. P1(b) led the researchers to predict that if learners were attending to lexical cues for tense, then those in the "no adverbial group" would perform poorly on a test that asks them to identify which events in the passage occurred in the past, which will occur in the future, and which are currently in progress. The prediction was supported. Subjects in the "adverbial group" were better able to determine the temporal reference of an event compared with those in the "no adverbial (verb inflection only)" group. Glass (1994) reports on a follow-up study in which he identified several good and poor learners who were subjects in the preceding "adverbials versus no adverbials" experiment. Glass reviewed their post-listening tests with them, replaying parts of the passage as they reviewed, and asked the subjects how they determined that an event took place in the past or not (e.g., probe: "You said that this event occurred in the past. How do you know that?") This introspective probe revealed that the subjects were relying on the lexical information (adverbials) and not on verb inflections to assign tense (e.g., subject response: Because [the speaker] said *el año pasado* ["last year"]). Important for this discussion is that unlike English, the Spanish past-tense morphemes are syllabic and receive strong stress; thus the results of the research just described cannot be so easily dismissed on the grounds that the grammatical items are "perceptually nonsalient."

Musumeci (1989) conducted similar research at the sentence level and used classroom learners of both Italian and French in addition to learners of Spanish. Musumeci asked her subjects to assign tense to input sentences delivered under one of four conditions.

1. verbal inflections accompanied by adverbials of time;
2. verbal inflections accompanied by typical teacher physical gestures (e.g., thumb over the shoulder to indicate past) but no adverbial marker of temporal reference;
3. verbal inflections accompanied by both an adverbial and a physical gesture; and
4. verbal inflections as the sole source of information about the tense of the sentence.

Again, P1(b) would predict that subjects receiving the lexical markers of tense in the input sentences would perform better than those who did not. Musumeci's results were similar to those reported in Cadierno et al. Subjects in the verbal inflections plus adverb group and those in the verbal inflections plus gestures plus adverb group consistently outperformed the subjects in the other two groups in which adverbs were absent in the input sentences. Her results clearly demonstrate that the presence or absence of a temporal adverbial was the significant factor determining correct tense assignment. This finding supports the primacy of lexical items over grammatical markers during input processing.

In short, there is evidence from both second language processing studies as well as learner-language research on first and second language learners to support principles P1, P1(a) and P1(b). The results of these studies suggest that learners' focal attention during input processing is on meaning, and precedence is given to lexical items for the conveyance of that meaning. When lexical items and grammatical features containing the same information compete for processing time, lexical items again have precedence.

Meaning and Form: Relative Communicative Value

In both first-language and second language literature, a fairly consistent picture has developed regarding the acquisition of verb morphemes. In English, -ing (progressive) is always acquired before -s (third person present), and -ed (past tense) is acquired somewhere in between (see VanPatten, 1984a, for more detail). Although one could argue that -ing is syllabic and therefore perceptually more salient in the input, we are left with the question of why -ed is acquired before -s. Both are verb-final, consonantal, and nonsyllabic (with the exception of one allomorph for each that contains a schwaed vowel). Clearly, something other than structural features is at work here. If one looks at the acquisition of Spanish, one finds that person-number inflections (-o, -n, -mos, -s, -is, -∅) generally are acquired before markings of adjective concordance (-o, -a, -s, -∅) (van Naerssen, 1981). Given the overall lack of structural differences between these two sets of morphemes (all are word final morphemes, both sets contain syllabic and nonsyllabic forms, none are stressed), something in addition to structural features is at work in acquisition. Although frequency may be a factor in determining the relative order of acquisition of a given grammatical feature (Larsen-Freeman, 1976), there is another possibility, one that falls out of our discussion of attention, detection, and meaning. Namely, it is the relative *communicative value* of a grammatical form that plays a major role in determining the learner's attention to it during input processing and the likelihood of its becoming detected and thus part of intake (VanPatten, 1984a, 1985b). We state this in the following principle.

P1(c). Learners prefer processing "more meaningful" morphology before "less or nonmeaningful morphology."

In this principle, "more," "less," and "nonmeaningful" refer to the communicative value that a grammatical feature contributes to overall sentence meaning. Communicative value refers to the relative contribution a form makes to the referential meaning of an utterance and is based on the presence or absence of two features: inherent semantic value and redundancy within the sentence–utterance. A form that can be classified as having inherent semantic value and is not a redundant feature of language, will tend to have high communicative value. For example, in English verbal morphology, -ing tends to have high communicative value for the following two reasons. First, it has inherent semantic value because it encodes progressive aspect, i.e., -ing = in progress. A second reason that -ing tends to be high in communicative value is that it is seldom redundant in naturally occurring discourse since, more often than not, no lexical information in the utterance co-occurs to provide cues to aspect. When we call someone on the phone we might say "hello" and then "What are you doing?" Likewise, when we see someone leaving we might ask "Where's she going?" In neither case do we add lexical information, for example "at this very moment," to the utterance. The sole conveyor of the semantic notion "in progress" is -ing, contributing to its relatively high communicative value. We can summarize this discussion by saying that in order to grasp the semantic notion of "in progress," the second language learner of English must process the verbal inflection -ing in the input. (Although we are concerned with grammatical form here, note that content words by their very nature can be considered to be high in communicative value.)

Other features of language will tend to have lower communicative value if they lack inherent semantic value or are redundant. Inflections on adjectives in languages like Spanish and Italian tend to be low in communicative value because they are both redundant and lacking in inherent semantic value. The -a in *blanca* does not carry any semantic meaning in the phrase *la casa blanca* "the white house." *Blanca* ends in -a because *casa* is of a particular grammatical class that requires this. Note also that this -a is spread across three words in the noun phrase, making it highly redundant.

Other grammatical features may have inherent semantic value but are low in communicative value because they are almost always redundant. The English verbal inflection -s, for example, has inherent semantic value since it encodes the semantic notion of third person singular, but it is also redundant because a subject noun-phrase is almost always obligatory in English syntax. Although colloquial speech allows a certain amount of subject-omission in English, for example, "Looks like rain," "Feels funny, heh?" the vast majority of sentences in English have explicitly marked subjects in them. In naturally occurring discourse, one would most assuredly hear "He loves me" and not "Loves me" as an answer to the question "How do you think he feels about you?" Given P1(a) and P1(b) and the primacy of lexical items in getting meaning from input, the learner is more likely to process the subject noun-phrase for person-number and not the verb form. Verbal -s thus is relatively low in communicative value, even though it can be said to have inherent semantic value.

Less clear cut cases are grammatical features such as tense markers. Clearly these have inherent semantic value since they encode temporal distinction. However, unlike third-person -s and Spanish and Italian adjective inflections, tense markers are not consistently redundant in an utterance. At the same time, unlike progressive -*ing*, they are not consistently nonredundant. Sometimes they co-occur with lexical indicators of time in an utterance, and sometimes they do not. In the following interchange, a co-occurring adverbial (represented in bold) is only mentioned in the first utterance.

Speaker A: *¿Por qué no viniste **anoche**?*
Speaker B: *Trabajé todo el día y no tuve ganas al salir.*
Speaker A: *¡Qué pena! ¡Lo pasamos tan bien!*
Speaker B: *¿Sí? ¿Qué hicieron?*

Speaker A: Why didn't you come **last night**?
Speaker B: I worked all day and I didn't feel like it after getting off.
Speaker A: Too bad! We had such a good time!
Speaker B: Yeah? What d'ya do?

At the present time, all we can say is that grammatical forms with semantic value but inconsistent redundancy will fall somewhere between items of high and low (or no) communicative value.

A scale of communicative value might be difficult to apply to all features of language, but in a recent study P1(c) was tested directly. Bransdorfer (1989) tested subjects' ability to process meaning and form simultaneously in Spanish when the form was either the preposition *de* or the definite article *la*, neither of which can be considered a content word. Bransdorfer argued that these two forms are structurally similar (both are syllabic and occur in roughly the same syntactic position in a sentence, i.e., before nouns), but he also argued that the preposition would carry greater communicative value than would the article. According to Bransdorfer, the preposition *de* had inherent semantic value as a signal of possession and, if absent, could pose problems of interpretation for a learner, for example, *El libro es Juan*, "The book is John" versus *El libro es de Juan*, "The book is John's." In the first case, the learner may not grasp whether John is the possessor of the book, the goal of the book (the book is for him), the subject of the book, and so on. On the other hand, the absence of the article *la* would *not* pose interpretation problems, e.g., *La pluma es verde*, "The pen is green" versus *Pluma es verde*, "Pen is green." He thus classified *la* as having lower communicative value.

Bransdorfer used a simultaneous attention task similar to that used in VanPatten (1990). Subjects heard a brief passage and were tested on its content by means of an immediate written recall in English. The subjects were divided into three groups: (1) those who listened to the passage only; (2) those who listened to the passage and also noted any occurrence of the preposition *de*; (3) and those who listened to the passage and also noted any occurrence of the article *la*. The results of Bransdorfer's experimentation revealed that there indeed was some kind of difference between the two grammatical items. There was no significant difference in recall scores between the passage only group and the passage plus *de* group. There was also no significant difference in recall scores between the passage plus *de* group and the passage plus *la* group. However, the scores of the passage plus *la* group were significantly lower than those of the passage only group. Attending to *de* while listening to the passage affected comprehension much less than attending to *la*. This suggests that as learners processed input for meaning, *de* was more likely to be attended to and detected than *la* and supports the construct of relative communicative value.

In his 1991 dissertation, Bransdorfer replicated his study using elements that carried strong stress: the lexical item *exámenes*, "exams" and the copular verb *está*, "is." The content lexical item would obviously be considered as having high communicative value since lexical items carry semantic value and in an utterance are generally not redundant *vis à vis* each other.

Bransdorfer classified the copular verb *está* as lacking inherent semantic value and thus lower in communicative value. His results revealed that attending to *exámenes* while listening to a passage posed no problem for comprehension but attending to *está* did result in a drop in comprehension.

Processing Grammatical Form of Little Communicative Value

The principles and supporting evidence presented so far suggest that attention is allocated during on-line processing according to relative communicative value. Processing capacity limits what a learner can attend to and detect when engaged in the ongoing and split-second process of deriving meaning from input. The internal processor seeks to carry out efficiently the task of getting information, and, in the early and intermediate stages of acquisition, the result is a tendency not to process or hold in working memory those items that do not contribute to meaning. However, L1 learners eventually do acquire most if not all features of adult language, and *some* L2 learners in input-rich environments do acquire many of the features of language that do not contribute to meaning (although in pidgins and fossilized speech, it is precisely those nonmeaningful features that tend to be absent). Putting aside socioaffective motivation for increased proficiency and focusing strictly on psycholinguistic aspects of learning, another principle suggests the reason for why all grammatical forms eventually may be acquired.

P2. For learners to process form that is not meaningful, they must be able to process informational or communicative content at no or little cost to attentional resources.

Recalling that one of the features of detection is that it is a heavy consumer of processing resources, the preceding principle suggests that grammatical form of little or no communicative value will be detected only when the resources required by detection to process meaning are not depleted. The prediction from this is that grammatical form of little or no communicative value will be processed much later in learners' development and subsequently will be acquired later than other grammatical form.

There is as of this time no solid experimental evidence that directly supports this principle. In one study, Leow (1993) hypothesized that simplification of input would result in decreased attentional demands on learners' processing of that input. Using a pre-test–post-test format, he measured the gains on a test of the present perfect and the present subjunctive in Spanish. Leow found that the subjects who read a simplified passage had greater gain scores compared with subjects who read an unsimplified passage. However, sampling errors suggest that the results may have been owing to existing differences in abilities between the simplified and unsimplified groups before receiving their passages. In any event, Leow's stimulus was written input, whereas our primary concern here is the processing of aural input.

In another attempt to investigate simplification and its possible affects on attention, Berne (1989) replicated VanPatten (1990), but simplified the listening passage by asking subjects in a pilot phase to tell her what sentences and parts of the passage were difficult to comprehend. Based on their comments, she simplified the passage by making some sentences shorter, changing some unknown vocabulary, and eliminating clauses. She then gave the listening passage two four groups as in the VanPatten study: focus on meaning only, focus on meaning plus a content word, focus on meaning plus a verb inflection, focus on meaning plus definite article. Her results, however, matched VanPatten's exactly: Learners' comprehension dropped significantly when focused on form and meaning, but not when focused on a content word and meaning. Simplification did not seem to help. Although surprising given that she had pilot feedback from subjects about the difficulty of the passage, Berne's findings may very well indicate that releasing attention to focus on nonmeaningful form may require a *great deal* of simplification of the input.

Another avenue to pursue regarding P2 would be to look at the effect of pausing. Blau (1990) found that of the three factors speed (slowing down the rate), complexity (reducing syntactic complexity and simplifying sentences), and pausing (adding brief pauses at natural breath group boundaries), pausing significantly improved the comprehension of most of her Puerto Rican and Polish learners of English as a second language. Slowing down the rate of speech or simplifying the syntax did not have the same degree of facilitative effect. A number of methodological questions render Blau's study more suggestive than definitive, but nonetheless the study points to a line of research that can help to investigate P2 more directly; less or nonmeaningful grammatical features should be more easily detected when the input contains pauses that allow for processing time.

Although it is reasonable to conclude that simplification decreases demands on attentional capacity, attentional capacity does not interact solely with communicative value to determine what is attended to in the input; attentional capacity is also affected by task demands of which processing time is a significant variable. Research needs to include studies in which pressure to perform the task is varied by amount of time available to do the task. It could be that even with simplified input, time pressure to comprehend may place sufficient demands on the learner such that attentional resources cannot keep up with the demands of the task. While we await studies on this issue, it is worth stating that even if processing time proves to be an important variable in determining attentional load for L2 input processing, processing time alone does not ensure attention to formal features of the input. In other words, processing time might be a necessary but not sufficient ingredient for attention to form in the input.

Looking at P2 in another way, if we assume that output reflects to some degree what has been processed in the input, there is some indirect evidence for P2. Recall that learners of English acquire verb morphemes in the following order:

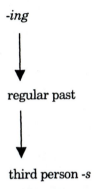

-ing

regular past

third person *-s*

with *-ing* being acquired fairly early on and *-s* being acquired relatively late. As discussed earlier, *-ing* possesses high communicative value and *-s* possesses little communicative value, whereas the past-tense marker falls somewhere in-between. Thus, the order of acquisition matches the input processing preferences of learners as the latter intersect with communicative value.

It is true that the example from English verbal inflections is compounded by frequency in the input as well as structural differences. *-ing* is found to be much more frequent than -s, for example, in spoken English. *-ing* is also syllabic rendering it more perceptually salient compared with nonsyllabic *-s*. One could easily conclude that languages might simply bias saliency (based on structural features) and frequency toward items of higher communicative value, and that factors other than communicative value and processing capacity account for acquisition orders. Until we see substantially more data from the acquisition of languages other than English, P2 will continue to be theoretically motivated, but not empirically supported. Given the demands that detection places on processing resources, it seems logical that the detection of grammatical form of little communicative value is inhibited by the allocation of processing resources to getting meaning from the input. (See also Schmidt, 1990, for some discussion here.) Detection of these grammatical forms will occur only if processing for meaning is relatively easy for the learner.

Summary

In our model of second language input processing, form-meaning mapping is affected by the limited capacity to process incoming data. Comprehension is seen as an effortful phenomenon that consumes a great deal of attentional capacity. Driven to get meaning, learners first allocate attentional capacity to detect content words in the input. Grammatical form conveying semantic information that also is encoded lexically will tend to not be detected; the learner instead relies on the lexical items for the semantic information. The learners' internal mechanisms will detect grammatical form early on only if it is relatively high in communicative value. Otherwise, grammatical form is detected over time only as the learner's ability to get meaning from the input is increasingly automatized (becomes more effort-free). This increasing automatization of comprehension releases attentional resources for the processing of form that was previously skipped (undetected). In Figure 2-2 we sketch a model of how processing based on limited resources works. As data enter the processors, the latter first search the input for content words. If resources are depleted, then the intake data delivered to the developing system essentially are content lexical items. If resources are not

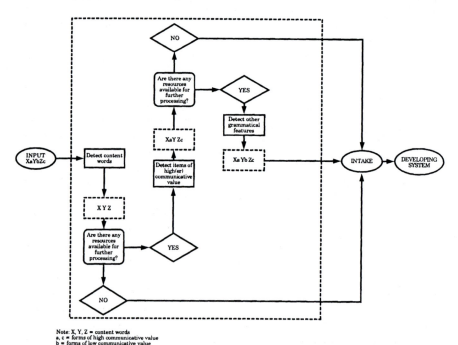

Note: X, Y, Z = content words
a, c = forms of high communicative value
b = forms of low communicative value

FIGURE 2-2. A model of processing grammatical form in the input based on attention and communicative value.

depleted, then the processors may make some form-meaning mappings using grammatical forms of high communicative value. If resources are depleted at this second stage of processing, then the intake will contain lexical items and some grammatical form. If the resources are not depleted, then further processing occurs. This time, the processors make form-meaning connections using grammatical form of lesser or little communicative value. The resultant intake thus will contain a number of features that were not processed previously. The different stages of processing, that is the points at which the processors determine whether or not resources are depleted, can be viewed as developmental in nature; early stage learners suffer resource depletion early in processing so that lexical items form the bulk of intake data. As the ability to attend to lexical items and connect them to meaning begins to use fewer resources, then detection of grammatical form of high communicative value may occur. As attention to and detection of these grammatical forms becomes easier and the demands on processing resources are lessened, then the learner can attend to and detect items of low communicative value.

Before moving on to our next discussion, we should acknowledge that, like any model, the one in Figure 2-2 is idealized and ignores individual characteristics of a given language. In addition, this is a model of input processing and not learning. A model of learning would attempt to capture accommodation of detected input (intake) and how the developing system restructures. Issues such as frequency in the input and semantic complexity of a form enter into a model of learning, but not one of input processing. The "job" of input processing is to detect linguistic data and make initial form-meaning mappings, even if they are incomplete or partial (i.e., the learner only maps one meaning onto a form). Thus, input processing provides the intake for further cognitive processing. Frequency is more relevant to the strength of long term store of linguistic data, that is, the strength of the form-meaning connections as they are stored in the developing system. Semantic complexity—whether a single form has various meanings or functions—again is more relevant to issues of long term storage. Once a form-meaning mapping is detected and subsequently stored, it is the job of the developing system to accept or reject a same form-different meaning mapping made available to it. As we shall see later in this chapter, in our discussion about the assignment of grammatical and semantic roles, it is certainly the case that the developing system may influence input processing itself by allowing or disallowing certain form-meaning connections to be made.

Finally, our model ignores issues of perceptual saliency for the time being. Perceptual saliency has been referred to earlier and involves whether or not a form has particular acoustic features that render it more salient in the speech stream than other grammatical forms. Acoustic features that presumably affect perceptual saliency are syllabicity (syllables are easier to detect than nonsyllables), stress (stressed syllables are easier to detect than weakly stressed or unstressed syllables), position in a word (beginnings and ends of words appear to be more salient than the middle parts of words except those carrying strong stress), and position in a sentence or utterance (utterance beginning and final positions are more salient that utterance internal positions, again except where strong stress is involved). (See Hatch, 1983, for a discussion of acoustic–perceptual salience.) It should be clear, then, that this model assumes that acoustic and perceptual factors are held equal. We will take up saliency again later.

ASSIGNING GRAMMATICAL AND SEMANTIC ROLES

The Principles

Not all of input processing is about attending to and detecting grammatical forms such as inflections and functors. When learners hear a sentence, they must also process it in order to assign semantic or grammatical roles to the words they hear. This means that they must assign roles such as agent and patient or subject and object to the nouns that they process. The present section will focus on this issue. The principles that we will examine are the following.

P3. Learners possess a default strategy that assigns the role of agent to the first noun(phrase) they encounter in a sentence. We call this the "first noun strategy."

P3(a). The first noun strategy can be overridden by lexical semantics and event probabilities.

P3(b). Learners will adopt other processing strategies for grammatical role assignment only after their developing system has incorporated other cues (e.g., case marking, acoustic stress).

We will show that in some languages, such as Spanish, P3 has major consequences in terms of the type of intake data that are fed to the developing system. We will suggest also that P3(b) may be developmentally late because of the intersection of P3 and the other principles examined in the previous section on cognitive aspects of input processing.

Meaning Once Again

In the previous section, we observed that learners are driven to get meaning from an utterance as part of comprehension. As we saw, this resulted in a series of principles in which the push to get meaning governed the processing of discrete elements in input sentences. However, meaning does not refer solely to the referential meaning encoded in words and grammatical form; meaning also refers to such things as *who* did what to *whom*. To grasp the meaning of an utterance, a learner must also determine what semantic or grammatical role a noun has. For example, as fluent comprehenders of English we would assign the semantic role of agent to the lion and the role of patient to the hunter in the following sentence.

(1) The lion killed the hunter.

If we heard the following sentence, however, we would reverse our assignment of semantic roles, this time assigning the agent role to the hunter.

(2) The lion was killed by the hunter.

Our correct interpretations are based on our mature knowledge of English syntax. The syntactic rules in our mental representation of the language do not allow us to assign, for example, the role of agent to the hunter in the first sentence. What do second language learners do when the appropriate mental representation has yet to be constructed? Somehow they must assign roles to the nouns they detect in a sentence. What principle or principles guide(s) them?

Research on second language learners has revealed a strong tendency for them to rely on a strategy by which the first noun of a sentence is tagged as the agent. We can state this as the following principle.

P3. Learners possess a default strategy that assigns the role of agent to the first noun (phrase) they encounter in a sentence. We call this the "first noun strategy."

Simply put, this means that regardless of the actual syntactic configuration of the sentence, learners interpret the first noun as the agent. Motivated by research in child first language acquisition (Bever 1970; Slobin, 1966), Nam (1975) showed how, for example, child and adult Korean learners of English as a second language incorrectly interpret passives. When presented with a sentence such as, "The lion was killed by the man," her subjects interpreted the sentence to mean that the lion did the killing and that the man was the entity that wound up dead. In other words, they incorrectly interpreted the sentence as "The lion killed the man."

Ervin-Tripp (1974) also reports on this processing strategy. She studied English speaking children attending a French-speaking school in Switzerland. She gave them passive sentences such as the following and asked them to act out the meaning of each sentence with toy animals.

(3) *La vache   a eté   chassée   par   le cheval.*
   "The cow   was   chased   by   the horse."

What Ervin-Tripp found was that her subjects tended to misinterpret the French passive sentences as actives, showing that the cow chased the horse rather than the other way around. She found this strategy in all ages of children that she studied. Of note here is that English and French form the passive in almost the exact same word-for-word way. Thus, the older children who clearly had knowledge of passive structures in English did not use this knowledge to interpret the French sentences. In other words, they did not rely on first language transfer to assign semantic roles.

A number of studies have been conducted in Spanish (Binkowski, 1992; Glisan, 1985; Lee, 1987; LoCoco, 1987; VanPatten, 1984b) on how learners of Spanish interpret sentences. Spanish has variable word order so that the following sentences are all possible, each meaning that the lion (*león*) killed (*mató*) the man (*hombre*).

(4) *El león mató al hombre.*
(5) *Al hombre lo mató el león.*
(6) *Mató el león al hombre.*
(7) *Mató al hombre el león.*

In addition, Spanish obligatorily places clitic object pronouns in front of finite verbs. Thus the following sentences are both possible, each meaning that the lion (*león*) killed (*mató*) him (*lo*).

(8) *El león lo mató.*
(9) *Lo mató el león.*

Using various research instruments and different input sentences, these studies on learners of Spanish show a strong tendency for them to misinterpret sentences in which the first noun is not the agent. Thus, (5) *Al hombre lo mató el león* is misinterpreted as, "The man killed the lion" instead of the correct "The lion killed the man." Sentences such as (9) *Lo mató el león* are misinterpreted as "He killed the lion" rather than the correct "The lion killed him."

In her study cited earlier, LoCoco also researched the sentence interpretation of second language learners of German. German marks nouns for case by inflection of determiners. Among her target sentences for comprehension, LoCoco included sentences in which the direct object preceded the verb as in the following example: *Den Lastwagen schiebt das Auto,* "The-ACC truck pushes the-SUBJ car" = "The car pushes the truck." There was a very strong tendency for learners to ignore the case marking cues and use word order to assign the grammatical-semantic roles.

Gass (1989) has also shown that English-speaking learners of Italian and Italian-speaking learners of English make use of the first noun strategy to process sentences. This is an interesting finding *vis à vis* first language transfer since research on native Italian-speaking adults suggests that other cues (e.g., animacy) are more important than word order for assigning semantic-grammatical roles (see discussion that follows on lexical semantics). MacDonald and Heilenman (1992) also provide evidence that adult English-speaking learners of French use a first noun strategy to assign semantic roles to nouns in sentences.

Research from various languages (both first and second) suggests that the first noun strategy may be a universal default strategy and not simply a matter of learners transferring knowledge of syntax from their first language during the act of comprehension. In one study of first language learners of Hungarian, Pléh (1989) showed that her subjects relied on this strategy, even though Hungarian clearly marks case which, in Bates and MacWhinney's (1989) terms, is a more reliable cue to semantic roles. Pléh gave her subjects sentences in various word orders (SVO, OVS, etc.) that are possible in Hungarian. She found that the Hungarian children do rely on something other than case marking to assign semantic roles, and concludes that "as the data from 178 children [ ] show there certainly is a strong bias toward using the first-noun-as-the-agent strategy " (p. 166). And when Pléh removed case markers from stimulus sentences, the first noun strategy was even more prominent.

That the first noun strategy may indeed be a universal default strategy in the beginning stages of acquisition is shown in the work of Bates and her colleagues (Bates & MacWhinney, 1989; Bates et al., 1984), even though they argue against it as a universal default strategy. In their Competition Model, word order is but one of a number of cues that languages may use to ensure proper assignation of semantic roles by comprehenders. They claim that no cue is universal and that speakers of a language develop biases toward one cue or the other based on the reliability, availability and cost of the cue (see MacWhinney & Bates, 1989, Chapter 1 for detailed discussion). Based on data such as those presented in Bates et al. (1984), they argue that adult speakers of Italian have a bias toward animacy as a cue and that English speakers have a bias toward word order. They also provide data to show that children learn these biases early on. However, these biases only hold in those cases in which the cues are put into conflict and does not mean that the first noun strategy is not a universal or default strategy. In every testing situation that Bates et al. report, the Italian speakers, children and adult, show evidence of *beginning* with a word order strategy and relying on animacy only in conflict situations. Thus, when given sentences such as the following in Italian

(10) The rock bit the giraffe

speakers of Italian select *giraffe* as the agent and not the first noun, *rock.*
Animacy here is in conflict with word order since inanimate things don't
bite. But when given sentences in Italian in which animacy is held constant
in the sentence, Italian speakers tend to select the first noun as the agent.

(11) The rock bit the leaf.
(12) The monkey bit the giraffe.
(13) The monkey the giraffe bit.
(14) Bit the monkey the giraffe.

In a certain sense, then, these data cannot be used to argue against a universal first noun strategy for assigning agency to a noun; they can only be
used to argue that speakers of some language develop additional strategies
or rely on additional cues in addition to word order. In short, everyone starts
out with a word order strategy but, depending on the language being
learned, may wind up with additional and, presumably, more reliable cues.

This leads us to another principle for assignment of semantic roles during input processing. We state it in the following way.

P3(a). The first noun strategy may be overridden by lexical semantics and
event probabilities.

Lexical semantics refers to the constraints on a situation imposed by the
semantics of the verb involved. The verb *kick*, for example, requires an animate being with legs to do the kicking. For this reason the sentence *He
kicked her with his ear* is anomalous as is the sentence *The snake kicked the
horse.* An event probability refers to the likelihood that a given situation
would exist in the real world, even though lexical semantics allows it. The
verb *correct* allows any animate being capable of instructional behavior to
correct someone or something else. However, of the two situations that follow, one is more likely than the other.

(15) The parent corrected the child for his behavior.
(16) The child corrected the parent for his behavior.

Most of us would agree that the first sentence is much more likely than the
second. It thus has a higher degree of event probability.

In first language acquisition and in adult native-speaker studies, lexical
semantics and event probability affect semantic role assignment. Bever
(1970) showed that children who misinterpret passives such as *The cow was
kicked by the horse* do not regularly misinterpret sentences such as *The pan-*

cake was eaten by the man. The lexical semantics of *eat* precludes an inanimate object eating an animate object in the real world, and thus children do not use the word order of the pancake sentence in assigning semantic-grammatical roles. Bavin and Shopen (1989) show that lexical semantics can override the first noun strategy for active sentences as well. They gave Walpiri speaking children a series of active sentences in which the lexical semantics allowed for either animate or inanimate nouns to perform or cause the action, for example, "trip" as in a person can trip another person or a log can trip a person. They also gave them sentences in which the lexical semantics allowed for only animate objects to perform the action. They found that the first noun strategy was operative in the first type of sentences, but was in much less evidence with the second type. In another part of their study, they gave the children sentences in which event probabilities would favor one noun over another as the agent. The children showed a very strong tendency in the earlier stages to use event probability rather than word order to assign the role of agent.

Both Gass (1989) and Issidorides and Hulstijn (1991) present data on the influence of lexical semantics on the first noun strategy for second language learners. Gass gave English-speaking learners of Italian and Italian-speaking learners of English sentences in which animacy conflicted with word order. That is, the first noun was an inanimate thing but the verb required an animate being as the agent, for example, *The rock bit the giraffe.* Her data were unequivocal in showing that both English- and Italian-speaking learners relied more on lexical semantics than word order to assign the semantic role of agent to the second animate noun in these kinds of "conflict" situations. Issidorides and Hulstijn tested second language learners of Dutch with various first languages on their comprehension of adverb-verb-subject-object sentences. They found a significant drop in assigning subject status to the first noun when it was inanimate and the second noun was animate.

Given the research from first language acquisition and the limited research from second language acquisition, it is reasonable to posit P3(a) as a principle that affects semantic role assignment. Although the first noun strategy may be a universal starting point for processing sentences, it seems that lexical semantics (and most likely event probabilities) will play a role in those situations in which the animacy of the first noun is at odds with the lexical nature of the verb.

In the previous section on attention and input processing, we suggested that the formal features that learners could attend to and detect in the input change over time as comprehension became less effortful. Concerning the assignment of semantic roles, what guides learners' processing of input also changes over time. We posit the following general principle.

P3(b). Learners will adopt other processing strategies for grammatical-semantic role assignment only after their developing system has incorporated other cues (e.g., case marking, acoustic stress, subject-verb agreement).

This principle is based largely on first language data, although there are a few studies from second language acquisition that are relevant. We will examine the data from first language acquisition first.

Languages vary as to whether they mark case or not and whether or not they have "free" word order. English is strongly SVO, whereas languages such as Spanish, Hungarian, Hebrew, Turkish, and Walpiri allow other orders, including SOV, VSO, OVS, and OSV. Significantly, most of the languages that allow other than SVO order mark nominal case in some way, usually marking nonsubjects. Spanish, for example, marks the accusative noun phrase with the preposition *a* when lexical semantics allows for the accusative noun to be equally capable of performing the action or event represented by the verb. The subject remains unmarked. (Although languages like those listed above may also mark nouns other than the direct object [patient] of a verb, we will limit ourselves to discussion of subjects and direct objects.) In the following examples, the verb *kill* allows for either *the man* or *the lion* to perform the act of killing. However, the verb *read* does not permit *the letter* to perform the action. (The marker *a* contracts with the masculine singular definite article *el* to form *al*.)

(17) *El señor   mató   al león.*
    "The man   killed   ACC-the lion."
(18) *El león   mató   al señor.*
    "The lion   killed   ACC-the man."
(19) *Al león   lo   mató   el señor.*
    "ACC-the lion   him   killed   the man."
(20) *Al señor   lo   mató   el león.*
    "ACC-the man   him   killed   the lion."
(21) *El señor   leyó   la carta.*
    "The man   read   the letter."
(22) **El señor   leyó   a la carta.*
(23) **A la carta   la leyó   el señor.*
(24) *La carta   la leyó   el señor.*

Hungarian, in contrast, inflects a noun with *-t* (or *-et* and *-ot*, depending on the stem of the noun) in order to mark accusative case. Like Spanish, the subject noun remains unmarked for case. The following sentences, taken from Pléh (1989), are all possible in Hungarian.

(25) *A macskát   átugorja   a kutya.*
    "The cat-ACC   jumps over   the dog."

(26) *A macska*   *átugorja*   *a kutyát.*
    "The cat   jumps over   the dog-ACC."
(27) *A fiú*   *a lányt*   *kergeti.*
    "The boy   the girl-ACC   chases."
(28) *A lányt*   *a fiú*   *kergeti.*
    "The girl-ACC   the boy   chases."

Research in first language acquisition has shown that first language learners must become sensitive to these cues to role assignment during the course of development (see, e.g., Bates & MacWhinney, 1989, pp. 59–70). That is, the cues are not immediately apparent to children and it is possible that the cues in one language are acquired earlier than the cues in another. A frequently cited example involves Turkish. Turkish children seem to have acquired the case marking system for correct role assignment by the age of two years (Slobin & Bever, 1982). In contrast, children acquiring Hungarian show evidence of correct role assignment much later, after the age of five years (Pléh, 1989). Children of French do not acquire adult-like cues based on animacy until well into adolescence (Bates & MacWhinney, 1989). These cross-linguistic differences are attributed to a variety of factors falling within the framework of the Competition Model (Bates & MacWhinney, 1989; McDonald & MacWhinney, 1989), which we will discuss in a later section. These factors largely are related to accommodation and restructuring of the child's developing system, and thus fall outside the scope of the present discussion on input processing. What is relevant, however, is that input processing itself is not guided solely by universal and invariant strategies; as language acquisition progresses, input processing is also guided by information contained in the developing system itself. That is, at some point, the knowledge stored in the developing system is utilized during on-line input processing, as learners either abandon the first noun strategy or utilize other grammatical information as well.

There is some evidence that the way(s) that second language learners assign grammatical and semantic roles during input processing develops over time like those of first language learners. McDonald & Heilenman (1992) report on second language learners of French and second language learners of English. In their study, both groups show gradual acquisition of sentence processing strategies that approximate those of native speakers with the second language learners of French showing a late development of the use of verb agreement as a cue to subject-object roles. In her report on learners of Italian and English, Gass (1989) shows that ESL learners of various first language backgrounds consistently rely on word order (the first noun strategy) for sentences in which lexical semantics plays no role. For sentences in which lexical semantics does play a role Gass found that the learners initially used both word order and the lexical semantics of the verb equally when interpreting the sentences. Overtime and quite gradually, the learners increasingly used word order only as the major cue to sentence processing.

The ability of second language learners to rely on cues other than word order may be slow when compared with such development in first language learners. The problem for second language input processing is the following. As we posited in the first section of this chapter, learners are driven by the push to get meaning. Lexical items are processed before grammatical cues when both express the same meaning. Grammatical and semantic roles certainly are a part of meaning since they are concerned with the who and the whom of events. These roles are expressed by nouns that are lexical items. As posited in the present section, learners use word order cues to assign grammatical and semantic roles based on the serial processing of nouns (lexical items). Thus, we can also say that learners prefer word order to grammatical cues for processing and assigning semantic roles to nouns in a sentence.

In the preceding scenario, the grammatical cues for role assignment are irrelevant from the point of view of the learner's internal processing mechanisms since the first noun strategy takes care of the bulk of the processing. Thus, these cues are initially low in communicative value. In a certain sense, they function like redundant markers (e.g., third person -s, Spanish adjective agreement) for the learner and we hypothesize here that they are ignored in the input for some time. There is no empirical research to support this argument, however. Experience with learners of Spanish shows that the accusative marker a is a late acquired item, often not showing up consistently in the output of graduating Spanish majors at the university level. Experience also shows that these somewhat advanced learners of Spanish may still have difficulty with verbs such as gustar, "to please" (Spanish has no equivalent of to like), which requires an almost obligatory OVS word order in Spanish, e.g., A Juan le gusta el helado, "ACC-John pleases ice cream." Experience further shows that learners of Spanish have difficulty in setting the null-subject parameter. In this latter case, many advanced learners of Spanish do not really have a null-subject system, but instead overtly mark subjects of verbs far more than a native-speaker would. Another persistent problem involves object pronouns and reflexive pronouns that in Spanish obligatorily precede finite verbs, for example, Lo veo, "ACC-him see-I," Se acuesta, "REFL- puts to bed-he." Errors such as *Lo viene for "He comes" and *Me hablo mucho for "I talk a lot" suggest that learners have misinterpreted the grammatical and semantic roles of these pronouns, using them as subject pronouns instead. These problems in output may very well be related to the first noun strategy that would mitigate against the detection of certain grammatical forms and the wrong function assignment to certain pronouns. This in turn would have subsequent learn-

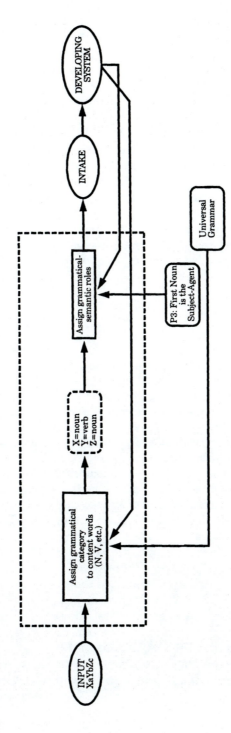

FIGURE 2-3. A model of grammatical-semantic role assignment in second language input processing.

ing effects for things such as the null-subject parameter. We leave these issues to future research.

Before summarizing, one final point deserves mention. When we say that learners use a first noun strategy, there is an assumption here that learners know what a noun is, a verb is, and so on. When learners incorrectly assign the subject-agent role to *macskát*, "cat" in an input string such as *A macskát átugorja a kutya*, they simultaneously show evidence of having parsed the sentence into noun phrases and verb phrases. This would suggest that learners have access to universal lexical categogies such as nouns, verbs, adjectives, and so on. We thus suggest that part of on-line input processing also involves first assigning words their referential meaning, e.g., *macska* = "cat," as well as their grammatical category, for example, *macska* = NOUN. In this way, input processing relies on certain knowledge sources such as Universal Grammar (which contains the abstract grammatical categories) and the semantic network of referential meanings contained in the developing system. Any model of input processing would have to include an indication of the processors making use of various knowledge sources.

Summary

In the previous section, we have examined the issue of grammatical-semantic role assignment during input processing. We have posited that word order is the starting point for second language learners with a heavy reliance on a first noun strategy. This strategy may be overridden in those cases in which lexical semantics does not conform with the role assignment. We also have suggested that the word order strategy may be overridden with time as the learners' developing system incorporates other cues to role assignment. These cues are utilized during on-line processing to help determine whether or not the first noun can indeed be assigned the subject case. Figure 2-3 summarizes the operation of these principles during on-line input processing. First, the processors assign grammatical categories (N, V, etc.) to the content words that are detected using information from UG (and, of course, the semantic meanings stored in the developing system). The processors then deliver this information plus the serial order in which the items occurred to that part of processing that assigns grammatical and semantic roles. In the early stages, the processors use the first noun strategy to assign grammatical roles. Later in second language acquisition, if the developing system contains other cues to grammatical and semantic role assignment, the processors will make use of these cues to assign grammatical roles and will override the first noun strategy if appropriate.

In Figure 2-4 we integrate role assignment into a more general model that includes the processing of grammatical form as described in the first

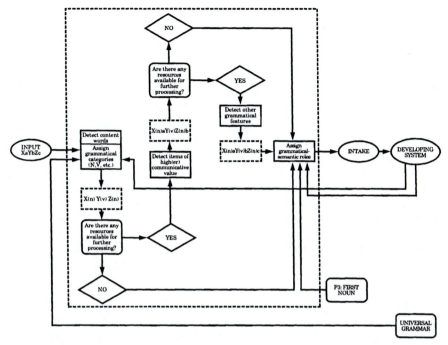

FIGURE 2-4. An integrated model of second language input processing for grammatical form and role assignment.

section of this chapter. The result is a more complete picture of on-line second language input processing.

OTHER ISSUES IN INPUT PROCESSING

There are a number of issues related to input processing that we have purposely ignored until now. Some of these issues relate to the conceptualization of attention as discussed in the first section. Others relate to issues of acoustic saliency and individual language characteristics as well as other models of language processing. Still others relate to some possible objections or confusions about input processing that can be caused by misinterpretation of the ideas expressed in this chapter. We will take each of these issues in turn.

Consciousness and Awareness

In previous publications (e.g., VanPatten, 1985b, 1990, 1994, 1995) I had explicitly linked attention to consciousness and awareness. In agreement with Schmidt (1990), I argued that processing grammatical form in the input required attention to form in the input. I viewed attention as having some degree of awareness or consciousness in it. Borrowing from Ceci and Howe (1983) and Posner and Snyder (1975), I suggested that "an operational definition of attention assumes some kind of consciousness in that the learner is either aware of the process or the product of attention. Because attention involves some degree of consciousness, it is capacity robbing" (VanPatten, 1994, p. 28). It was this model of attention that informed my previous research.

More current research in cognitive psychology, as described in Tomlin and Villa (1994), suggests that awareness or consciousness is not a necessary component of some aspects of attention. In reviewing work by Posner and his colleagues (e.g., Posner & Petersen, 1990; Posner & Rothbart, 1992), Tomlin and Villa conclude that

> none of the central components of attention—alertness, orientation, or detection—require awareness, either to operate or as the result of processing. Detection is the most related to awareness, but there is considerable evidence indicating that information can be cognitively detected even though the individual is not aware of it having occurred (p. 193).

In spite of these recent developments, it is not clear that this conclusion is readily applicable to second language acquisition. Most if not all studies in attention and learning use adults, and none of these studies focuses on either first or second language acquisition, although a few involve language phenomena. In lexical priming studies, such as Marcel (1983), as cited by Tomlin and Villa, adult native-speaking subjects read a word such as *nurse* on a computer screen. Studies reveal that subjects read the word more rapidly when appearing immediately after the semantically related word *doctor* as opposed to the more semantically unrelated word *actor*. However, subjects cannot indicate above chance that they have seen the word *doctor* prior to being asked to read the word *nurse* suggesting that they do not have any awareness of the word *doctor*. Such studies are used to conclude that detection (in this case, detection of a lexical item) does not necessarily involve awareness.

What is important here is that the research uses adult native speakers. These adult native speakers already have a fully developed semantic and lexical system in addition to well-rehearsed retrieval mechanisms that they use when processing incoming language. The particular lexical items they process in the above described studies are words (and not grammatical items, by the way) that they have already learned and are well entrenched in the long term store that comprises their lexical-semantic network. In short, *the subjects aren't involved in the processing of novel form-meaning mappings;*

they are being asked to perform with knowledge that they already have. This is quite different from the *initial* form-meaning mappings that a second language learner must detect and learn. The lack of awareness of adult native-speaking subjects in studies such as lexical priming could be a *result* of learning and extended language use. We cannot conclude from these studies that initial processing in the input that is crucial to building the linguistic system in second language acquisition occurs without awareness.

In the same vein there are studies cited to indicate that learning of finite state grammars and structural sequences happens without awareness. Finite state grammars contain a set of letter nodes (e.g., X, Y, Z, S, T, U) connected by one-way arrows. The direction of the arrows depict in what serial order the letters can be colocated. These grammars can thus generate strings of letters that function as "input sentences" to adult subjects who subsequent to the input phase are given a surprise grammaticality judgment task with correct and incorrect strings of letters (e.g., Carlson & Dulany, 1985; Carr & Curran, 1994; Dulany, Carlson, & Dewey, 1984; Reber, 1976). Subjects perform better than chance on surprise grammaticality judgment tasks of letter stings but often are unable to articulate why a string is grammatical or not. I have reviewed the problems in applying these kinds of results to second language acquisition elsewhere (VanPatten, 1994) and will briefly (re)state my argument here. Internalizing the ordering of letters in a string is not the same as the very complex processing and learning of new form-meaning mappings in a second language. Finite state grammars do not encode any kind of meaning (the letters are simply letters and do not represent any real world meaning), they do not contain inflections, functors, and other surface features of language, they do not contain movement rules and varying word orders, and the studies based on them involve purely visual processing during the learning phase. Even Carr and Curran (1994, p. 207) admit that the application of such studies to discussions on second language acquisition must be viewed with some caution and can only serve as a focal point for discussion at this time.

In addition to these criticisms of finite state grammar, we are faced with the same problem in applying the results of these studies to second language acquisition that we faced earlier. The subjects are not second language learners acquiring new form-meaning mappings; they are adults learning to match already known forms (letters) to serial patterns. However, second language learners are processing new forms and in some cases mapping these on to new meanings such that their task cannot be deemed equivalent to those experienced by subjects in the experiments on cognitive psychology.

Because of these problems in interpreting cognitive research on consciousness and awareness and applying them to second language acquisition, I have opted to eliminate references to consciousness and awareness altogether from the principles and the model of input processing developed in this chapter. Although my position is that awareness is probably a part of input processing at least initially, it is not necessary for positing the strategies described in previous sections. What *is* necessary is the concept of limited processing capacity. Recall that the model for attention to and detection of form in the input developed in this chapter relies on the notion that detection consumes attentional resources. In research on structural learning, Carr and Curran (1994) report that, even though structural learning seems to happen outside of awareness with adults in nonlanguage tasks, it does require focal attention—which is synonymous with detection in their discussion. When subjects' must perform a concurrent task, their ability to learn the structural patterns—and recall that these patterns are believed to be learned without awareness by the majority of researchers—is impaired if not made impossible. Carr and Curran also cite the effects of a limited capacity on learning finite state grammars. Furthermore, Dienes, Broadbent, and Berry (1991) performed an experiment in which subjects were given the usual experimental exposure to input letter-strings generated by the grammar but were asked to perform a concurrent task. The results revealed a marked decline in the subjects' post-treatment ability to judge strings as grammatical or not suggesting that their implicit processing of the letter strings during the learning phase was impaired. (See Whittlesea & Dorken, 1993, for additional related research.)

We argued earlier that the research on awareness based on finite state grammars is not necessarily applicable to second language acquisition because of the inherent complexity of natural languages and the form-meaning mappings that must occur. Here, however, the results of studies such as those conducted by Dienes, Broadbent, and Berry (1991) are relevant. If subjects reveal a limited capacity to process rather simple strings of letters, logically it follows that to process new forms and perform all the mental operations required to map form onto meaning in second language acquisition must be at least as taxing if not more. As Carr and Curran (1994) state

> The syntax of natural language presents a very complicated hierarchic organization with many interrelated conditional rules on what elements can combine with one another. Therefore, it seems a plausible guess that natural language learning taxes the system's ability to keep track of context more severely than learning the model grammars used in structural learning tasks... syntactic learning may well require, or at least benefit from, focal attention (p. 224).

Thus, while we sidestep the issue of consciousness and awareness in the present chapter, we do so without loss to our model of input processing. It seems that detection during processing consumes attentional resources and that we can test this with or without imbuing it with any degree of consciousness (cf., McLaughlin, 1990). We leave the issue of consciousness and awareness to future research in both cognitive psychology and second language acquisition.

Form Versus Meaning

Very often, discussions of second language acquisition pit form against meaning. This has led to discussion in both second language acquisition circles as well as language teaching circles of "attention to form" and "attention to meaning" (see, e.g., the discussion in Garrett, 1991). In positing P1, P1(a–c) and P2, it is conceivable that some would interpret these principles as dissociating meaning and form as well. However, since input processing is concerned with how learners make form-meaning connections when attending to input, the question cannot be whether learners attend to meaning *or* to form. The question is under what conditions they can *attend to both* and how attention to form and meaning develops over time. As stated in VanPatten (1990)

> What is critical to keep in mind is that the issue of attention to form in the input is only an issue when the input is communicative in nature, i.e., it carries information to which the learner is supposed to attend. This is the kind of input that is typically found in nonclassroom settings and in certain kinds of classroom methodologies, e.g., the Natural Approach. While humans may indeed direct [conscious] attention to form in and of itself, the question is not whether they can do this; the question is *whether or not they can do this while they process the input for meaning* (p. 288, emphasis original).

For this reason, the principles sketched out in this chapter suggest conditions under which form-meaning mappings can occur; they do not suggest that form and meaning necessarily are separate. In addition, they do not suggest that early stage learners should not have attention directed toward form via instruction; they only suggest that certain kinds of form are more difficult to detect than others when learners are left to their own devices. In the next chapter, we will see just how learners' attention can be directed toward form in the input without loss of meaning.

Operating Principles

For those familiar with the work on Operating Principles in first language acquisition (e.g., Peters, 1985; Slobin, 1973, 1985), a number of questions may arise. To what extent are the principles described in the present chapter different from those described in the child first language literature? Are there principles in first language acquisition that are applicable to second language acquisition?

To be sure, there is some relationship between first language Operating Principles and the second language input processing principles posited in this chapter. In previous work (e.g., VanPatten, 1984b) I have acknowledged the role of first language acquisition research in suggesting research questions for second language acquisition. However, Operating Principles and the principles described in the present chapter are not equivalent. Let us take, for example, Slobin's well known Operating Principle "Pay attention to the ends of words." Slobin posits this Operating Principle to account for the fact that nominal case inflections (noun-endings) are acquired earlier by Turkish children than case marking prenominal markers are by Serbo-Croatian children. He suggests that children are guided by a principle that directs their attention to the ends of words rather than to functors and pre-posed markers. Although his data certainly support this claim, he posited this Operating Principle to account for cross-linguistic differences and we certainly could apply the Operating Principle to second language acquisition as well. We could hypothesize that English speakers learning Turkish will acquire its case marking system before English-speakers will acquire the same for Serbo-Croatian. Such principles, then, could easily be incorporated into the present model and researched.

What is different about Slobin's Operating Principles and the principles outlined in this chapter is that Slobin mixes input processing strategies with both learning and production strategies in his list of Operating Principles. "Pay attention to the ends of words," for example, is a principle that guides child input processing. An example of a principle that guides production is "Avoid interruption or rearrangement of linguistic units." This principle accounts for the fact that learners prefer canonical orders in their output and is reflective of how the internal system has stored and organized the intake data. As such, the principle has little to do with actual on-line sentence processing and instead refers to what learners do with the data after it has been initially processed. In our model of second language input processing, the principles are restricted to input processing alone. We are not concerned with principles of learning, i.e., principles directly related to the accommodation and restructuring of intake data (see Figure 1-3 in Chapter 1), although we will touch on this issue in Chapter 5. Likewise, we are not concerned with issues of on-line sentence production.

Peters (1985) also posits what she calls Extraction and Segmentation heuristics. Based largely on phonological cues in the input, Extraction heuristics explain how children may initially perceive and process units in the input larger than the word while treating the unit as a word. For example, one of Peters' Extraction heuristics is the following.

EX: SILENCE. An extractable unit is bound by silence.

This heuristic accounts for how children initially perceive and attend to chunks of language that are bookended by pauses. Segmentation heuristics then allow children to subsequently break off pieces of extracted units as they begin to make internal comparisons. These comparisons result in novel data. One example of a segmentation heuristic is the following.

SG: REPETITION. Segment off subunits that are repeated (in terms of segmentals or rhythm or intonation) within an Extracted unit and store them separately.

Thus, a child who may have initially extracted *Wheresyour* as a unit based on repeated input strings such as "Where's your nose?" "Where's your eye?" "Where's your truck?" and so on, may encounter new input containing sentences such as "Where's the spoon?" "Where's the dog?" In this case, according to Peters, the child is equipped with segmentation heuristics to compare the internal unit *Wheresyour* with the new *Wheresthe* to determine that *Wheres* is an even smaller unit. In positing Extraction and Segmentation heuristics, Peters can account for why children's units of speech may be different from those of adults and certainly different from those of linguists.

Although Peters' extraction heuristics certainly seem to be concerned with input processing, her segmentation heuristics often are related to learning rather than to processing. That is, they are concerned with how the child accommodates new intake data and how the developing system subsequently restructures itself. Her extraction principles dovetail nicely with the principles outlined in the present chapter, but are driven more by issues of perceptual (read "acoustic") salience than they are by issues of attention and capacity. There can be no doubt that acoustic and perceptual saliency interact with the principles outlined in the present chapter. For example, let's take two forms of relatively equally low communicative value from the perspective of the second language learner. One, however, happens to occur in the middle of words and generally receives weak stress; the other occurs at the ends of words and sentences and carries strong stress. Our principles would predict that these forms would be processed and acquired later than forms with consistently high communicative value. However, Peter's heuristics would predict that the form occurring at the ends of utterances would get extracted and segmented before the one occurring in the middle of words. Her heuristics, however, would not make any prediction based on relative communicative value when perceptual saliency is held constant. Our principles could not make any prediction about earlier or later processing when communicative value was held constant and perceptual saliency was varied. Thus, the principles in the two different models are complementary and not mutually exclusive.

The conclusion to be reached is that a fully articulated model of input processing would need to include both principles based on attention and capacity as these interact with communicative value and perceptual saliency. For the purposes of the present book, we have chosen to focus on the former—along with the principles involved in grammatical and semantic role assignment. Careful research needs to be conducted to investigate the intersection of cognitive aspects of input processing in second language acquisition with acoustic-perceptual saliency.

The Role of First Language Transfer

First language transfer has a long history of debate in second language acquisition theory and research. Most views of transfer focus on issues in learning (accommodation and restructuring) or in speech processing (how the first language influences the way in which learners put utterances together). It is not immediately clear how first language transfer may influence input processing, but we can speculate by looking at the issue of word order.

First, it is widely accepted in second language research that first language transfer is constrained by certain principles of learning (e.g., Andersen, 1983; Hyltenstam, 1987; White, 1989). In one view, transfer is triggered only when crucial similarity between the first and second language becomes apparent to the learner or the learner's developing system creates a rule that is similar to a rule in the first language. (See, e.g., Andersen's Transfer to Somewhere in Andersen, 1983.) In this view, the developing system is vulnerable to "seepage" from the first language system as the internal mechanisms make comparisons.

For example, as posited in a previous section, learners tend to assign the first noun of an input string the role of grammatical subject or semantic agent. This means that they will assign the role of object to the second noun. The intake data that they are feeding to the developing system would suggest that the language they are learning is invariantly SVO. Thus, the accommodation and restructuring mechanisms involved in learning would create a rule that says, "This language is SVO." Now let's imagine that learners with first languages like English that have invariant or systematically canonical SVO word order are learning a language like Spanish that has variant word order. The "natural rule" created in the developing system through the normal course of learning has set up a situation ripe for first language transfer; the SVO rule of the first language strengthens the SVO rule of the developing system.

In our model of input processing (see Figure 2-4) we have set up a developmental situation in which learners' processing mechanisms begin to check their assignment of grammatical and semantic roles against the rules contained in the developing system. In this way, the first noun strategy may still operate but the results of its operation are checked against the knowledge (rules) stored in the developing system. If the developing system contains an SVO rule with no other cues to assigning grammatical and semantic roles to nouns, and this SVO rule has been strengthened by the first language, then we see that transfer operates in an indirect way in second language input processing. We will touch upon first language transfer again in Chapter 5 as we explore the relationship between input processing and Universal Grammar.

The Competition Model

The Competition Model has become a recognized framework for examining both first language use (adult comprehension of sentences) and first language acquisition. Only recently have scholars begun to explore the potential of this framework for second language acquisition (e.g., Gass, 1989; McDonald & Heilenmann, 1992) and in the previous sections we have referred to it on occasion. The question that arises is whether or not input processing and the principles established in this chapter fall within the Competition Model, especially since so much work in the Competition Model has been concerned with grammatical and semantic role assignment. In order to answer this question, a brief overview of the Competition Model is in order.

The Competition Model is a functionalist model designed "to capture facts about comprehension, production and acquisition of language by real human beings, across a variety of qualitatively and quantitatively distinct language types" (Bates & MacWhinney, 1989, p. 3). The principal idea of the Competition Model is that humans must develop form-function mappings for language use, that each language possesses "cues" that are utilized during on-line comprehension and production. Adults use these cues, whereas children must learn what they are.

The Competition Model has one major predictive construct: cue validity. In simple terms, cue validity refers to the degree to which a cue helps a comprehender in making correct interpretations during on-line sentence comprehension. Cue validity itself contains three components. The first is availability, which simply means the degree to which a cue is available when you need it. Subject-verb agreement is not a readily available cue in English since verbs do not inflect for person-number, except for present-tense, third person singular. Subject-verb agreement is a readily available cue in languages like Spanish and Italian. The second construct is reliability and represents the degree to which a comprehender can count on a cue in making correct interpretations. In English, word order is about 100% reliable for assigning semantic and grammatical roles to nouns. Word order is less reliable in Spanish. The third construct, conflict validity, refers to the degree to which a cue renders a correct interpretation when it is in conflict with another cue. Conflict situations are infrequent in natural language situations but form the staple of the research paradigm for the Competition Model. In languages like English, conflict can never happen with word order since other cues (subject-verb agreement, case marking on nouns) are generally unavailable. Conflict can happen in languages likes Spanish as we saw in a previous section of this chapter. Word order ("the first noun is the subject") may be in conflict with case marking ("but the first noun is case marked with *a*") and so the comprehender must use one cue or the other to assign grammatical and semantic roles.

Although the Competition Model accounts for adult on-line comprehension issues, Bates and MacWhinney apply the model to first language acquisition. Within the Competition Model, children's acquisitional problem is one of learning about cue validity. Over time, children must internalize what the best and most valid cues are for all comprehension situations in the language. According to the model, children are equipped with learning mechanisms that compute weights and strengths of cues in the developing system so that they wind up with the appropriate adult system (McDonald, 1989; McDonald & MacWhinney, 1989). In this way, the child develops an internal system that serves as a template or resource against which the internal processors judge incoming cues.

From this brief description, it should be clear that the Competition Model is an attempt to link knowledge sources with on-line processing. In terms of the principles presented in this chapter for second language input processing, the Competition Model can be seen as complementary and useful for understanding how P3(b) develops; it cannot tell us how learners *first detect* and process grammatical form in the input. The Competition Model simply assumes that grammatical form is processed by child first language acquirers. Recall that P3(b) says the following: Learners will adopt other processing strategies for grammatical role assignment only after their developing system has incorporated other cues (e.g., case marking, acoustic stress). This principle says that learners make use of their developing system (a knowledge source) for on-line processing as they progress through acquisition. However, the formal cues that this system might contain are an indirect result of P1(a–c) and P2. Thus, the Competition Model cannot tell us how the cues are initially detected and made available for those mechanisms that compute cue validity for the developing system. This is not intended as a criticism, since the Competition Model is not meant to be a model of attention and detection.

We conclude this section, then, by saying that the Competition Model fits within our P3(b) and may prove to be a useful framework for discussion of the eventual accommodation of new intake data and restructuring of the developing system in second language acquisition. However, because of the relative incompleteness of second language acquisition for most learners, we cannot assume that learners attend to and detect cues in the input in the same way that this is assumed for child first language acquisition. For this, we need to develop other frameworks for understanding how learners initially attend to and detect grammatical form in the input, and the principles and model developed in this chapter seek to do just that.

CONCLUSION

In this chapter, we have posited principles of second language input processing based on two major questions: What guides the way(s) in which learners process grammatical form in the input? How do learners assign grammatical-semantic roles to nouns? Using the construct of attention and limited capacity processing, we have posited a set of processing principles regarding how learners process grammatical form. Using first and second language research on grammatical and semantic role assignment, we have posited a set of principles related to how learners determine subjects and objects of verbs. Along the way, we have attempted to make links between input processing and language acquisition. That is, input processing shapes the intake data available for accommodation by the developing system. As intake data are accommodated and restructuring occurs, learners' developing systems take shape. We also have compared our model to others and found complementarity rather than opposition. We also acknowledged that perceptual salience and its role in input processing must, at some point, be incorporated in a model of input processing.

The question we ask now concerns the usefulness of a model of input processing for second language instruction. Curriculum developers and instructors have tended to shy away from theory since little direct connection seems to be made between theory and actual practice, at least in terms of grammar instruction. The Monitor Model, the Acculturation Model, Universal Grammar, and other models and linguistic theories may help instructors understand language acquisition in general but they offer few insights into how to best facilitate the acquisition of grammar in a day-to-day situation. In the next chapter, we will examine how knowledge of input processing can lead to very concrete applications to the classroom.

chapter **3**

PROCESSING INSTRUCTION

INTRODUCTION

In the previous chapter we outlined a set of principles for input processing that inform second language acquisition theory about how learners attend to input data. In the present chapter we will examine processing instruction, a type of explicit grammar instruction that initially was motivated by the critical role of input processing in acquisition. Our purpose in doing so is to provide background on the instructional treatment researched in the various studies summarized in Chapter 4.

In this chapter we will first review the motivation for processing instruction. By examining traditional output-based grammar instruction, we will see that traditional instruction is not informed by general second language acquisition theory. Our conclusion will be that traditional instruction is not psycholinguistically motivated. Next we will describe processing instruction in some detail, focusing mainly on the nature of "structured input" activities. We will see that underlying all structured input activities is the push to get learners to make form-meaning mappings in order to create grammatically richer intake. Subsequently, we will briefly compare the nature of comprehension-based language teaching with processing instruction. Since there is potential for reductionism, our purpose here is to point out that processing instruction cannot simply be equated with comprehension-based language teaching.

MOTIVATION FOR PROCESSING INSTRUCTION

A General Model of Second Language Acquisition

In Chapter 1 we emphasized the importance of communicative or meaning-bearing input in second language acquisition. Successful language acquisition simply does not happen without it. We also saw that learners process the input to create intake, and that intake are the data that can be accommodated by the developing system. We sketched out a simple model of these sets of processes and display it once again in Figure 3-1.

In examining the model in Figure 3-1 we see that the major chain of events for acquiring a particular form go from left to right. First, learners get input containing that form. If it is processed, that form becomes intake data. As intake data, the form is a candidate for accommodation by the developing system. If accommodated, then the form becomes part of the developing system with possible restructuring in other parts of the system depending on the nature of the form and the (transitional) stage at which the system finds itself. If accommodation or restructuring occurs, the form can be tapped by the output processing mechanisms responsible for production.

What is relevant for the present discussion is that the acquisition of formal features of language *begins* with input and input processing. For a learner to be able to eventually access and use a form in output in an unmonitored way, that form must be part of the developing system. How did that form get there? Again, formal features of language enter the system via the processes represented by I and II in Figure 3-1. This discussion sets the stage for an examination of the basic problem with traditional instruction.

The Problem with Traditional Instruction

For most traditional approaches to grammar instruction, it is fair to say that most if not all grammar instruction is output-oriented. This is particularly true of foreign language classrooms in the United States. Classroom learners get explanations about rules and paradigms from instructors and materials,

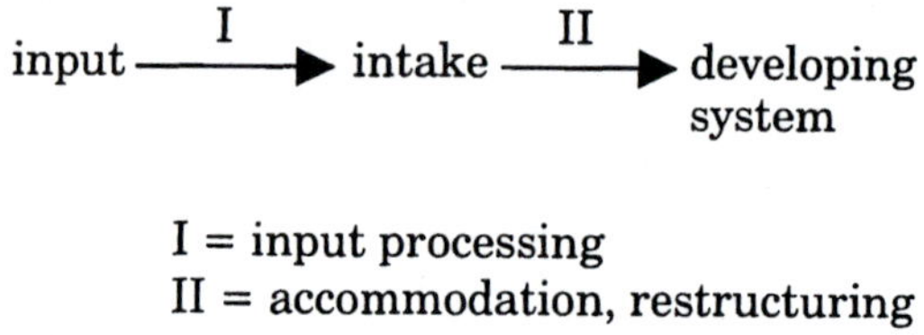

$$\text{input} \xrightarrow{\text{I}} \text{intake} \xrightarrow{\text{II}} \text{developing system}$$

I = input processing
II = accommodation, restructuring

FIGURE 3-1. Input processing and intake in second language acquisition.

and then they practice these rules and paradigms via various output exercises and activities. The reader may recall from Chapter 1 that over 25 years ago, Paulston (1972) codified a particular sequencing of oral grammar practices. She suggested that grammar-based oral practice should proceed from mechanical to meaningful to communicative exercises. She also emphasized that mechanical practice (pattern drills) were a necessary first step in the internalization of the rules and forms of the second language. Couched within the dominant language learning theories of the 1950s and 1960s, Paulston's claim seemed sensible. Behaviorism, with its focus on observable behavior, habit formation, and immediate feedback, served as the cornerstone for the development of audio-lingualism and its promulgation in language teaching. Oral production was the observable behavior, correct oral production and avoidance of grammatical errors were the habits to be formed, and on-the-spot error correction served as the immediate feedback. Regardless of major theoretical shifts in cognition, linguistics, and the vast research undertaken in child language acquisition since the early 1960s which clearly has dispelled any application of behaviorism to first language acquisition, and in spite of the research on second language acquisition since the early 1970s, language instruction has continued to regard grammar learning as largely oral. At the time of writing of this book, Paulston's hierarchy for grammar practice is alive and well, as evidenced by the type of grammar instruction and practice found in the vast majority of textbooks used to teach foreign languages in this country. For example, one of the most popular Spanish college-level textbooks on the market today follows this particular approach to grammar instruction as evidenced by by the following lesson on object pronouns.

Direct Object Pronouns
▸ A direct object noun is often replaced by a direct object pronoun. The following chart shows the forms of the direct object pronouns.

Singular		Plural	
me	me	*nos*	us
te	you	*os*	you (informal)
lo	you (masc), him, it (masc)	*los*	you (masc), them
la	you (fem), her, it (fem)	*las*	you (fem), them

▸ Direct object pronouns agree in gender and number with the noun to which they refer.

Quiero el libro.	*Lo quiero.*
Quiero los bolsos.	*Los quiero.*
Llamo a Teresa	*La llamo.*
Llaman a las chicas.	*Las llaman.*

▸ Direct object pronouns are usually placed immediately before the conjugated verb.

¿Dónde ves a Jorge y a Adela?	Where do you see Jorge and Adela?
Los veo en la clase.	I seem in class.
¿Quieres la blusa, Mili?	Do you want the blouse, Mili?
Sí, la quiero.	Yes, I want it.
[explanation continues]	

Práctica

1. *El (La) olvidazo (a).* You and your roomate have forgotten who is doing what.
   Modelo: *¿Quién va a comprar los sandwiches?* (Who is going to buy the sandwiches?)

   Tú los vas a comprar. (You are going to buy them.

   1. *¿Quién va a llamar a las chicas?*
   2. *¿Quién va a buscar el hielo?*
   [3–6 continue in the same vein]

Práctica comunicativa

2. *Vamos a la playa.* With some friends, organize a day at the beach.
   Modelo: *¿Quién lleva la bolsa?* (Who's taking the bag?)
      Yo la llevo. (I'm taking it.)
   1. *¿Quién hace los sandwiches?*
   2. *¿Quién compra los refrescos?*
   [3–6 continue in the same vein]

As can be seen, a traditional structural explanation of the form and the rules that govern it is followed immediately by mechanical output practice. (Interestingly, the so-called *práctica comunicativa* is also a mechanical practice.) As one more example of this traditional approach, the reader is invited to examine the following two parts of a "study tip" given to the learners regarding verb forms in Spanish.

▸ Practice conjugating several -*ar* verbs in writing first. Identify the stem, then write the various verb forms by adding the present tense endings listed on page XX. Once you have done this, say the forms you have written out loud several times.

▸ Next, you will need to practice -*ar* verb conugations orally. Create two sets of index cards. On one, write down the subject pronouns listed on page 36 (one per card). On the other set, write some of the -*ar* verbs you have learned. Select one card from each set and conjugate the verb with the selected pronoun.

The focus on output and mechanical practice as the means by which the linguistic system develops should be evident in the cited examples. What is clear from this approach to grammar instruction is that the accommodation and restructuring of the developing system is seen to happen because of practice, not because of exposure to language samples in the input.

From the previous discussion the major problem with traditional approaches to grammar instruction emerges: There is a mismatch between the widely accepted role of input in second language acquisition and the output-based and often mechanical nature of grammar instruction and practice in much of language teaching. Input is input and output is output and the question arises as to just where the communicative meaning-bearing input is to be found in traditional grammar instruction. Output practice is not the data upon which the developing system relies for growth. Nor is the explanation about grammar provided by the instructor or the textbook. Explanations are information about language, but they are not the language data themselves.

A major motivation for processing instruction, then, comes out of our critical examination of traditional approaches to grammar instruction. However, there is another motivation as well. As claimed in VanPatten (1993), classrooms are becoming increasingly communicative and input-rich. Instructors are encouraged to use the second language in a variety of ways to communicate information. They are encouraged to have learners engage in tasks in which the learners themselves must communicate information and use language meaningfully (e.g., Lee & VanPatten, 1995; Nunan, 1989; Savignon, 1983). In addition, instructors are encouraged to get more comprehensible input into the class and to make comprehension an essential component of the classroom and the curriculum (e.g., Krashen, 1982; Krashen & Terrell, 1983). The problem in these directions for language teaching is that traditional grammar instruction just doesn't seem to fit. Lockstep and largely mechanical in nature (especially in foreign language classrooms in the United States), traditional grammar instruction conflicts with the more fluid, learner-centered, and content-based nature of communicative classrooms. And indeed, output drills just don't seem to go with input-based classrooms. Thus, a second motivation for rethinking grammar instruction concerns congruence. Although not completely necessary, many of us would like to have the various instructional components of our classroom blend together in some harmonious whole.

The question to be asked is the following: If a traditional output-based approach to grammar instruction is incongruent with current theory about second language acquisition, then would an input-based approach to grammar instruction be better? Of no surprise, our answer is yes, *but only if the instruction takes into consideration the nature of input processing.* We turn our attention now to a description of the components of processing instruction.

THE NATURE OF PROCESSING INSTRUCTION

Overview

The goal of processing instruction is to alter the processing strategies that learners take to the task of comprehension and to encourage them to make better form-meaning connections than they would if left to their own devices. To achieve this, processing instruction has three key components: (1) explanation of the relationship between a given form and the meaning it can convey; (2) information about processing strategies, showing learners how natural processing strategies may not work to their benefit; and (3) "structured input" activities in which learners are given the opportunity to process form in the input in a "controlled" situation so that better form-meaning connections might happen compared with what might happen in less controlled situations. Component (1) often may resemble some of the information provided to learners in more traditional approaches to grammar instruction, whereas components (2) and (3) are unique to processing instruction. Since these components form part of the treatment used in the research studies we will review in the next chapter, it is important to discuss them here. We will take each of these components in turn, spending the majority of our time in examining component (3), structured input.

Explanation

As in most approaches to focus on form, processing instruction provides learners with some information about grammatical form. Structural properties of a feature are given and rules are described, but what is most important is that the explanation attempts to link form and meaning. In the following example, taken from the instructional materials used in VanPatten and Cadierno (1993), which in turn were based on materials used in VanPatten, Lee, Glass, and Binkowski (1992), the explanation of object pronouns in Spanish informs students of how pronouns encode meaning (semantic and grammatical roles) in addition to the structural aspects of object pronouns.

Sample Lesson

An object of a verb is a grammatical concept different from a subject. An object generally is defined as a thing or person on which an action or process is performed. Thus, in the sentence "John writes letters," "John" is the subject and "letters" is the object (the action of writing is performed on the letters). In the sentence "She has an idea," "She is the subject (pronoun) and "idea" is the object (the thing on which the process of "having" is performed). What is the subject and what is the object of the verb miran in the following sentence?

Los padres miran a los hijos.

Right. *Padres* is the subject (parents are the ones doing the watching) and *hijos* is the object (the things being watched). Did you notice that *hijos* is preceded by *a*? This *a* is called "personal *a*" and is used to mark objects of a verb. You will learn more about it later. What is the subject pronoun that corresponds to *padres*? *Ellos, él,* or *nosotros*?

_____ *miran a los hijos.*

Right again. *Ellos. Los padres* is the subject noun and *ellos* is the subject pronoun. Subject pronouns are already familiar to you.

yo	*nosotros/as*
tú	*vosotros/as*
usted	*ustedes*
él/ella	*ellos/ellas*

In Spanish (and English), not only are there subject pronouns, but there are also object pronouns:

The parents watch *them* (that is the kids).
Los padres los *miran (es decir, a los hijos).*

Here are the first set of subject and object pronouns that you will become familiar with.

	Pronouns	
	Subject	**Object**
First person singular	*yo* *Yo comprendo a mi hermano.* (I understand my brother.)	**me** *Mi hermano* **me** *comprende.* (My brother understands me.)
Second person singular	*tú* *Tú comprendes a los abuelos.* (You understand your grandparents.)	**te** *Los abuelos* **te** *comprenden.* (Your grandparents understand you.)
First person plural	*nosotros* *Nosotros comprendemos* *a los parientes.* (We understand our relatives.)	**nos** *Los parientes* **nos** *comprenden.* (Our relatives understand us.)

Me, te and *nos* are objects of the verb in the right hand column. In the first example, who is being understood? Me. In the second, who is being understood? You. In the third, who is being understood? Us.

There are two things to keep in mind about object pronouns:

1. They are placed in front of conjugated verbs.
2. They indicate on who or what the action–process is being performed, not who or what performs the action–process.

We will not discuss explanation further and turn our attention to a unique aspect of processing instruction: informing learners of the potentially problematic outcomes of processing strategies.

Informing Learners of Processing Strategies

In addition to information on how a form or structure works, learners receive clues or hints in processing instruction about paying attention to form in the input. Recall from Chapter 2 that learners utilize a first-noun strategy to assign grammatical and semantic roles such that the first noun they encounter in the input string is assigned the role of subject or agent. This leads to wrong assignment in sentences in Spanish such as the following

(1) *La   sigue   el señor.*
    Her-ACC   follows   the man.
    "The man follows her."

Learners typically assign the pronoun *la* the subject role and misinterpret the sentence as "She follows the man."

In processing instruction, this tendency to rely on word order alone is pointed out to learners, albeit in a nontechnical manner. After explanation about object pronouns they are then informed of something like the following:

> What can get tricky in correctly understanding a sentence is that often you will see or hear a sentence in which the order is object-pronoun-verb-subject, just the opposite of what you would expect!
>
> *Nos invitan las chicas a cenar.*   (The girls are inviting us to dinner)
>
> *No te comprende el profesor.*   (The professor doesn't understand you.)
>
> So be careful and don't make the mistake of interpreting the object pronoun as the subject of a sentence! (from VanPatten, Lee, & Ballman, 1996).

Sometimes this information is repeated in an activity so that learners are reminded of the problems in processing input. The following sample direction lines come from an activity in a sequence of activities used in VanPatten and Cadierno's (1993) study.

> Actividad A. Select the picture that best corresponds to the sentence. (Keep in mind that Spanish does not follow a rigid subject-verb-object word order and that object pronouns may go before a conjugated verb or at the end of an infinitive.)

In her research on processing instruction and past tense in Spanish, Cadierno (1992, 1995) informed students of how to pay attention to tense cues in the input. After an explanation of how the past tense is formed, Cadierno provided her subjects with the following:

> Preterit (past tense) forms are often accompanied by temporal adverbs that indicate that the action of the verb occurred in the past. Here you have some of these past temporal adverbs: *ayer* (yesterday), *anteayer* (day before yesterday), *anoche* (last night), *la semana pasada* (last week), *el lunes, martes, etc., pasado* (last Monday, Tuesday, etc.), *hace un mes* (a month ago), etc.

> However, although these adverbials are a good clue to know that an action has occurred in the past, they are not always present in the sentences that you encounter. This is the reason why it will be important for you to recognize past tense verb forms. And remember, the best clue you have is the spoken stress in the vowel of the endings of the verb (from Cadierno, 1992, p. 318).

The last point is particularly important since the instructional explanation itself contrasted the stress patterns of the present tense with those of the past. Present tense verb forms in Spanish almost always carry stress on the verb stem or root. Past tense forms carry stress on the verb ending.

What Cadierno attempted to do in these instructional lines, then, is shift the focus of attention during input processing off of the temporal adverbials and direct it to the verb endings themselves. However, one thing is to tell learners to do this; another is to provide them opportunities to do so. One thing is to tell learners not to mistake object pronouns for subjects and another is to give them opportunities to make correct grammatical and semantic role assignments. We now turn our attention to activities used in processing instruction.

Structured Input

Activities in processing instruction utilize what is best termed "structured input." "Input" refers to the fact that during the activities, learners do not produce the targeted grammatical form or structure. Instead, they are engaged in actively processing input sentences. The term "structured" refers to the fact that the input has been manipulated in particular ways; it is not free flowing communicative discourse, although it is meaning-bearing.

The activities in processing instruction (at least as it has been used in the empirical studies that we will examine in Chapter 4) also use a mixture of referentially oriented activities and affectively oriented activities. By referentially oriented activities we mean activities during which the content focus of the input sentences is not on the learners but on some other third person(s). These activities are used to check that the learners are actually processing the form. In these types of activities, there is a right or wrong answer that reveals whether or not the learners have made correct subject and object role assignment. In Figure 3-2 are two examples of referential activities used in VanPatten and Cadierno (1993) on the teaching of object pronouns and word order.

As can be seen in the first activity *(Actividad G)* in Figure 3-2, learners must choose between two English glossings to show that they have assigned subject and object roles correctly to the sentences that they read. In the second activity *(Actividad H)*, learners must choose between two glossings to show that they have assigned subject and object roles correctly to the sentences that they hear. (Other examples of referential activities can be seen in the sample lesson laid out later in this chapter.) Referentially oriented activities can be used at any time in a lesson but are particularly critical at the beginning of a sequence of activities. Because they entail either right or wrong answers, they can serve as a sort of starting point in a sequence of activities to ensure that learners are making correct form-meaning mappings. These particular activities have a mix of SVO and OVS type sentences, and thus purposely push learners to rely on cues other than word order (the first noun strategy) to get the propositional meaning of each sentence.

Unlike referentially oriented activities, affectively oriented activities have no wrong or right answer. Learners indicate agreement–disagreement, true for me–not true for me, check boxes in surveys, in short, they provide indications of their opinions, beliefs, feelings, and personal circumstances. In our initial work on processing instruction (VanPatten & Cadierno, 1993), we included affective structured input activities because general communicative language teaching incorporates affectively oriented activities on a regular basis. Thus, we were attempting to tie processing instruction to some of the more general tenets of communicative language teaching, which include an emphasis on meaning and on learner-centeredness. Figure 3-3 contains two examples of affectively oriented activities used in VanPatten and Cadierno (1993). In these activities, learners provide information about themselves. Note that the sentences are simple and relatively easy to process. In addition, sentences do not follow SVO order so that learners must attend to the meaning of the sentence and make correct form-meaning mappings in order to complete the activity successfully, as they did in the previously described referential activities.

Actividad G: Pronombres Select the correct interpretation of the sentence. Keep in mind that Spanish has flexible word order and doesn't necessarily follow subject-verb-object order like English.

1. *Mi hermana me llama frecuentemente.*
    Who calls whom?
    a. I call my sister.   b. My sister calls me.

2. *¿Te escriben tus padres?*
    Who writes to whom?
    a. Do you write to your parents?   b. Do your parents write to you?

3. *No nos escuchan los padres.*
    Who doesn't listen to whom?
    a. Parents don't listen to us.   b. We don't listen to parents.

4. *Me conocen bien mis hermanos.*
    Who knows whom well?
    a. My siblings know me.   b. I know my siblings.

Actividad H: ¿Objeto o sujeto? Match each sentence you hear with one of the statements below. Remember that Spanish does not always follow subject-verb-object word order!

1. a. ☐ A man is calling me.
   b. ☐ I am calling a man.
2. a. ☐ My parents visit me.
   b. ☐ I visit my parents.
3. a. ☐ I follow others.
   b. ☐ Others follow me.
4. a. ☐ We are greeting a friend.
   b. ☐ A friend greets us.
5. a. ☐ Our relatives don't understand us.
   b. ☐ We don't understand our relatives.
6. a. ☐ A friend is inviting you to dinner.
   b. ☐ You are inviting a friend to dinner.
7. a. ☐ The professor is watching us.
   b. ☐ We are watching the professor.
8. a. ☐ María is looking for you.
   b. ☐ You are looking for María
9. a. ☐ Juan believes us
   b. ☐ We believe Juan.

FIGURE 3-2. Referentially oriented activities used in VanPatten and Cadierno (1993).

The point of this chapter is not to provide detailed instructions in how to prepare appropriate structured input activities for processing instruction. This is done in significant detail in Lee and VanPatten (1995, Chapter 5). Again, given that we are setting the stage for understanding the research described in the next chapter, it is important to highlight a set of guidelines that have begun to inform the construction of structured input activities used in processing

Actividad J: Los parientes. What are things that relatives do to us? They can bother us, visit us, criticize us, love us, and so on.

Paso 1. Read each statement and select the ones that you think are typical.

Los parientes...
    a. ☐ *nos molestan.*
    b. ☐ *nos critican.*
    c. ☐ *nos ayuden* (help).
    d. ☐ *nos visitan.*
    e. ☐ *nos quieren* (**querer** = to be fond of).
    f. ☐ *nos* _____.

Paso 2. Now select the alternatives that you think make sense.

Los parientes...
    a. ☐ *pueden molestarnos aunque* (although) *no deben.*
    b. ☐ *pueden criticarnos aunque no deben.*
    c. ☐ *pueden ayudarnos aunque no deben.*
    d. ☐ *pueden visitarnos aunque no deben.*
    e. ☐ *pueden querernos aunque no deben.*
    f. ☐ *pueden* _____ *nos aunque no deben.*

Actividad L: Mis padres. How do you interact with your parents? Indicate whether or not each statement applies to you.

	SÍ, SE ME APLICA	NO, NO SE ME APLICA
1. *Los llamo con frecuencia por teléfono.*	☐	☐
2. *Los visito los fines de semana.*	☐	☐
3. *Los visito una vez al mes.*	☐	☐
4. *Los abrazo cuando los veo* (**abrazar** = to hug).	☐	☐
5. *Los comprendo muy bien.*	☐	☐
6. *No me importan.*	☐	☐
7. *Los aprecio* (appreciate) *mucho.*	☐	☐

FIGURE 3-3. Affectively oriented activities used in VanPatten and Cadierno (1993).

instruction. These guidelines were first reported in VanPatten (1993) and are subsequently elaborated on in Lee and VanPatten (1995, Chapter 5). For our purposes, we will review them briefly. It should be noted that only the second, fifth, and sixth guidelines are related in any particular way to issues in input processing and psycholinguistics as we have discussed them in Chapter 2. The others were developed for practical and experiential reasons as described in each case. It should also be noted that these are guidelines, not maxims. Variations in their application from lesson to lesson may occur.

Guidelines for Structured Input Activities

The first guideline for developing structured input activities is the following.

1. *Teach only one thing at a time.*

What this means is that paradigms and rules can and should be broken down into smaller parts. In traditional instruction of the past tense in Spanish, for example, it is typical to give learners all the forms of regular verbs for all three verb conjugations in one large paradigmatic chart. After studying and memorizing this chart, learners practice all the forms via output drills. For processing instruction, we have advocated breaking up paradigms and actually "building" them during the course of the lesson. Thus, learners might initially learn about third person singular past tense verb forms in Spanish and work through some structured input activities before going on to another person in the verb paradigm. In VanPatten and Cadierno (1993) and Cadierno (1995) this is precisely what was done—and the length of the lesson was not increased when compared to time spent on explanation and practice during traditional instruction; "full coverage" of the grammatical points was attained in both traditional and processing instruction in the same amount of time.

The second guideline that we have developed for structured input activities is the following.

2. *Keep meaning in focus.*

What this means is that the input strings must encode some meaning that the learner is required to attend to and respond to in some way. This particular guideline was motivated by my initial work with students of language teaching. When instructed to develop input-based grammar activities, I have noticed that a number of students create activities in which it was possible to complete the activity and not once connect meaning to form. For example, one student created an activity in which the learners had to scan a short paragraph and circle all the past tense endings. She was correct in that the learners did not have to produce anything, but this and other activities like it demonstrate that teachers may not understand the definition of communicative meaning-bearing input or at least forget about it when developing activities for processing instruction. They have also forgotten that input processing involves making form-meaning mappings, not just noticing form in and of itself. This guideline, then, serves as a reminder that the purpose of structured input activities is to push learners to make form-meaning connections. If meaning is absent or if learners do not have to pay attention to meaning to complete the activity, then there is no enhancement of input processing.

The third guideline for developing structured input activities is

3. *Learners must do something with the input.*

This guideline means that learners must be engaged actively in processing the input sentences and must demonstrate this by responding to the input sentences in some way. They may state agreement or disagreement, say "Yes, that applies me," or "No, that doesn't apply to me," complete a survey, select alternatives (e.g., a, b, c, or d), offer a name, make an association, in short, indicate in some way that they have attended to the meaning contained in the input sentence(s). This guideline was motivated again by my work with teachers-in-training who could not distinguish between talking at and talking with learners. The guideline was formulated so that they might better understand that input does no good if the learner is not paying attention to it. Asking learners to respond to the input in some way helps to insure that they are indeed paying attention.

A fourth guideline that was developed is

4. *Use both oral and written input.*

This guideline was established to account for individual differences. Experience has suggested that some learners benefit to different degrees from the mode of input. Some say they like to "see" the language, whereas others do not make this claim. A combination of oral and written input is a response to these claims and is not tied directly to the principles of input processing outlined in Chapter 2.

A fifth guideline addresses sentential vs. discourse-level input. It states

5. *Move from sentences to connected discourse.*

This guideline means that early activities should involve sentence level input such as those activities for object pronouns reviewed in the preceding section. Connected discourse (listening to conversations, monologues) should be reserved for later in the lesson. The rationale for this is that learners have a better chance at focusing on and detecting the targeted form in sentences as opposed to connected discourse when first engaged in structured input activities. As mentioned in VanPatten (1993), connected discourse may hinder learners' initial processing of the targeted form because of their limited capacity to process incoming data. Connected discourse may not give learners sufficient "processing time" as the sentences in the discourse occur one after the other to form a larger narrative or text. The result may be that much of the input is "noise" and the learners may have difficulty in attending to and detecting the relevant grammatical item. In Chapter 2 we reviewed the difficulty experienced by learners in the experiment reported in VanPatten (1990). Comprehension of content suffered severely when learners also attempted to attend to form. Terrell (1991) also suggests the same, noting that learners may not be able to "bind" forms from discourse-level input and instead use strategies that allow them to simply comprehend (get the gist) and respond in appropriate fashion. Since we want learners to attend to content (meaning) *and* form, starting a sequence in processing instruction with discourse-level input does not seem optimal.

The sixth and final guideline is perhaps the most important since it makes explicit reference to input processing. It says

6. *Keep the psycholinguistic processing strategies in mind.*

This guideline is intended to ensure that learners' attention is appropriately guided during structured input activities. In the examples referred to in Figures 3-2 and 3-3, for example, the activities systematically push learners to not rely on the first noun strategy. In both the initial referential activities and the subsequent affective activities, learners quickly face the fact that the first noun may not be the subject, thus, developing other form-meaning mappings for semantic and grammatical role assignment. These activities, then, keep in mind what the learners' natural processing strategy is and the input is structured to alter learners' reliance on the strategy.

Like several other guidelines, guideline 6 was borne out of my work with teachers-in-training. It seems that some novice attempts to create structured input activities reflect an understanding that the activities should be input-based but do not reflect an understanding of what learners are doing when processing input. For example, I have seen teachers-in-training create past-tense activities in which every single utterance contains a past tense adverbial. As pointed out in Chapter 2, the presence of the adverbial actually detracts from the role of the tense marker on the verb since learners prefer to process the adverbial (lexical item) as opposed to the grammatical form (inflection) when both encode the same semantic information. I have also seen teachers-in-training who create activities with object pronouns in Spanish but do *not* include activities in which the learner must assign the grammatical role of object to the first (pro)noun in the sentence. In other words, they create activities in which the first noun is always the subject, thus reinforcing the first noun strategy. I have seen teachers and teachers-in-training create structured input activities in ESL for the continuous present (e.g., "I am writing a book these days," "My spouse is teaching a course on reading research this semester") in which many of the input sentences contain adverbials such as "these days," "this semester," and so on. Thus, learners' attention is detracted from the meaning of the continuous present since the same meaning is encoded in the adverbial phrases. And I have seen teachers-in-training create activities in French for adjective agreement in which learners do not need to pay attention to adjective endings while making form-meaning connections.

In short, I have seen well-intentioned teachers create interesting meaning-based input activities but these activities do not attempt to alter the processing strategies of learners. These activities do not systematically push learners to direct attention (detection) during input processing to targeted forms.

To drive the point of guideline 6 home, we will compare two activities. Spanish requires that all adjectives inflect for number and gender. Under many naturally occurring situations, adjective endings can go undetected since head nouns contain the same information. In the phrase *la mujer española* ("the Spanish woman"), *mujer* ("woman") is singular and feminine. The adjective marker *-a* is redundant and of low communicative value; the learner does not have to attend to it to get the meaning of the phrase. Likewise, in *dos hombres americanos* ("two American men"), the adjective marker *-os* is redundant, since *hombres* is masculine and *dos* signals plurality. Hence, the adjective ending carries little communicative value.

Based on the preceding, we can determine that only one of the following two activities actually works at getting learners to attend to the adjective marker for possible form-meaning connections. The first one, A, was produced by a teacher-student enrolled in a language teaching class. B, is adapted from Lee and VanPatten (1995, p. 101). (Note: *ella* = she; *es* = is; the adjectives are purposefully cognates for the benefit of the reader who knows no Spanish. In addition, adjectives ending in *-o* generally are masculine, whereas adjectives ending in *-a* are generally feminine.)

A. Listen as your instructor reads a sentence about Hillary Clinton. Decide whether what you hear is true or not.

sí	*no*	
❑	❑	1....
❑	❑	2....
❑	❑	3....
❑	❑	4....
❑	❑	5.... etc.

(Instructor reads the following: 1. *Ella es dinámica.*; 2. *Ella es agresiva.*; 3. *Ella es egocéntrica.*; 4. *Ella es honesta.*; 5. *Ella es divorciada.*; etc.)

B. Listen as your instructor reads a sentence. First, decide whether the sentence is about Bill Clinton or Hillary Rodham Clinton. Then, decide whether you agree with the statement or not.

agree disagree

❑	❑	1.	❑ Bill	❑ Hillary
❑	❑	2.	❑ Bill	❑ Hillary
❑	❑	3.	❑ Bill	❑ Hillary
❑	❑	4.	❑ Bill	❑ Hillary
❑	❑	5.	❑ Bill	❑ Hillary

etc.

(Instructor reads: 1. *Es dinámica.*; 2. *Es agresivo.*; 3. *Es egocéntrica.*; 4. *Es honesta.*; 5. *Es respetado.*; etc.)

Of the two preceding activities, only B considers learners' allocation of attention during on-line processing. In activity B, learners first have to determine who is being talked about in each sentence. The only way to determine this is to attend to the endings of the adjectives. Thus, learners are pushed to connect form (adjective ending) with meaning (in this case, masculine vs. feminine). Second, learners must agree or disagree. In this way learners are not only attending to form and connecting it to its specific meaning, but they are attending to the meaning of the entire sentence as well. Activity A does not do this. Note how the activity does not encourage learners to attend to the adjective endings. Each sentence contains an explicit subject pronoun, *ella*, that encodes feminine-singular. Recall (again) that learners prefer to process lexical items as opposed to grammatical markers when both encode the same semantic information. In short, the entire activity is set up so that learners do *not* have to attend to and detect adjective endings. It does not encourage form-meaning mappings.

A Sample Lesson

Because the purpose of the present chapter is to describe processing instruction so that the reader is better able to interpret the research presented in Chapter 4, we offer here part of the processing instruction that was used in VanPatten and Cadierno (1993). This sequence focuses on third person (other forms of object-pronouns were presented in a previous part of the lesson—see guideline 1). It was used as the set of materials for the second day of instruction in a two-day long instructional treatment. (Note: the materials were not actually published in the VanPatten and Cadierno study. They do appear, however, in VanPatten, Lee, Glass, & Binkowski, 1992; Cadierno, 1992.)

Sample Lesson

The most difficult object pronoun system for students of Spanish is the set of third person object pronouns.

Subject	Object
Ella *besa a Juan.*	*Juan* la *besa.*
(She kisses John.)	(John kisses her.)
El *besa a María.*	*María* lo *besa.*
(He kisses Mary.)	(Mary kisses him.)
Ellos *observan a Marcos.*	*Marcos* los *observa.*
(They observe Mark.)	(Mark observes them.)
Ellas *observan a Carlitos.*	*Carlitos* las *observa.*
(They observe Charlie.)	(Charlie observes them.)

Keeping in mind that Spanish has flexible word order, what do you think the following sentence means?

Lo escucha Roberto.

Right. Roberto listens to him.

Un Vistazo: El arte de besar

In the following cartoon, who is kissing whom?
_____ *Lo besa la mujer.* _____ *La besa el hombre.*

Actividad A. Select the picture that best corresponds to the sentence. (Keep in mind that Spanish does not follow a rigid subject-verb-object word order and that object pronouns may go before a conjugated verb or at the end of an infinitive.)

☐ a   ☐ b
1. *Sus padres lo llaman por teléfono.*

☐ a   ☐ b
2. *Las invita Manuel al cine.*

☐ a   ☐ b
3. *La abuela lo escucha.*

☐ a   ☐ b
4. *Lo saluda la niña.*

☐ a   ☐ b
5. *El chico la busca.*

Actividad B. Indicate whether or not each statement about your parents applies to you. Share your responses with a classmate.

Sí, me   No, no
aplica   me aplica.

_____   _____   1. *Los llamo con frecuencia por teléfono.*
_____   _____   2. *Los visito los fines de semana.*
_____   _____   3. *Los visito una vez al mes.*
_____   _____   4. *Los abrazo cuando los veo.*
                       (*abrazar* = to hug)
_____   _____   5. *Los comprendo muy bien.*
_____   _____   6. *Los ignoro completamente.*
_____   _____   7. *Los aprecio mucho.*

Did you notice that there are no explicit subject nouns or subject pronouns in each sentence? Because the *yo* form of the verb can only refer to *yo*, no subject pronoun is needed. All of the sentences are of the simple word order object pronoun-verb.

Actividad C. Select a female relative of yours (*madre, hermana, tía, abuela, prima*, etc.) and write her name below. Which of the statements describes how you feel about her?

Pariente: _____   *Nombre:* _____
_____ 1. *La admiro.*
_____ 2. *La respeto.*
_____ 3. *La quiero mucho.*
_____ 4. *Trato de imitarla.*
_____ 5. *La detesto.*
_____ 6. *La* _____? _____.

Now select a male relative and do the same!
_____ 1. *Lo admiro.*
_____ 2. *Lo respeto.*
_____ 3. *Lo quiero mucho.*
_____ 4. *Trato de imitarlo.*
_____ 5. *Lo detesto.*
_____ 6. *Lo* _____? _____.

Compare with two other people. Did you select the same relative(s)? Did you mark the same items?

Actividad D. Listen to each statement and select the appropriate picture.

1.   ☐ a   ☐ b

2.   ☐ a   ☐ b

3.   ☐ a   ☐ b

4.   ☐ a   ☐ b

5.   ☐ a   ☐ b

(For activity D, the instructor reads the following statements.
1. *Lo llama Juan por teléfono.*
2. *La escucha el señor.*
3. *La abraza la mamá.*
4. *Los saluda la mujer.*
5. *El niño la mira.*

Un vistazo: Una mala relación

An article *"El caso del hermano posesivo"* appeared in a magazine targeted for teenagers. Read the excerpt for general meaning. Some vocabulary is provided to help you out, but it's not necessary to read and understand every word. The activities that follow are based on this reading.

seguir (to follow)
asustarse (to become frightened)
aconsejarse (to advise)
soltar (to leave alone, release)
jurar (to swear)
el colmo (the last straw)
paz (peace)

DEBATE

Un drama familiar muy común: ella se siente dominada, perseguida por su hermano mayor (que puede ser menor, pero con aires de grandote) y no sabe cómo zafarse de él. Alicia y Manuel so el caso típico.

ALICIA CUENTA SU PARTE

"Manuel es muy posesivo. No me deja respirar. Cada vez que voy a salir, me pregunta con quién, a dónde voy, qué vamos a hacer… A veces me sigue. Lo juro. Cuando un chico viene a visitarme Manny lo interroga y él se asusta. El colmo: mis padres me dejaron ir con unas amigas a un concierto de Bon Jovi… y Manuel les aconsejó que uno de ellos fuera con nosotras, para supervisarnos. Por poco lo mato. De veras, mi hermano es peor que mis padres. Por eso peleamos mucho. Le he dicho más de mil veces que él no es mi papa y que me deje en paz. Pero Manuel no me suelta."

Actividad E. For each paso of this activity, work in pairs.

Paso 1. Find the following in the reading:
me dejaron ir
me pregunta
me sigue
no me suelta
viene a vistarme

In each instance, Alicia is saying that someone is doing something to her or for her. Can you identify the subject of each verb?

Paso 2. Find the following in the reading:
lo juro
lo mato
lo interroga

Who is the subject of each verb? Who or what does each *lo* refer to?

Un vistazo: Manny responde

In the following selection, Manuel responds to his sister's claims. Read it now for general meaning. Then do the activities that follow.

no queda más remedio	(no choice is left)
había visto	(had seen)
confiar	(to trust)
mentir	(to lie)

MANNY HACE UNA ACLARACION

"No quería decirlo, pero no me queda más remedio. Si vigilo a mi hermana, es porque me ha dado motivos para sospechar de ella. En varias ocasiones la sorprendí con un tal Sergio, que es uno de esos rebeldes sin causa con la reputación por el suelo. Una vez le dijo a mis padres que iba al cine con las amigas y después un buen amigo me contó que la había visto en el cine... pero con Sergio. ¿Cómo puedo confiar en mi hermana si miente a todos en la casa? Ella no conoce a los chicos. Ese tipo sólo busca una cosa. Y yo no quiero que a mi hermana le suceda nada 'feo.'"

Actividad F. For each paso in this activity, you should first work alone and then share your responses with someone else.

Paso 1. Find all the uses of a third person object pronoun. To whom or what do they correspond? What is the subject of each verb next to which you found each pronoun?

Paso 2. Which of the following best describes Manny's feelings for his sister?
____ *La quiere mucho.*
____ *La admira.*
____ *La detesta.*

Paso 3. Which of the following does Manny probably do on a Friday night if his sister goes out?
____ *La sigue para ver lo que hacer y con quién.*
____ *La deja en paz porque es una adulta.*
____ *La espera en casa.*

Recall that Spanish has the object marker *a*.

*Los padres miran **a** los hijos.*
*Llamo **a** mis padres.*

This object marker has no equivalent in English but is important in Spanish since it provides an extra clue as to who did what to whom. Since Spanish has flexible word order, the *a* reminds you that even though a noun appears before the verb it doesn't have to be the subject!

A María la llama Juan.
A María Juan la llama.
(John calls Mary.)

Note that when an object appears before the verb, the corresponding object pronouns must also be used. If you think that this is redundant, it is! But redundancy is a natural feature of languages, right? (Hint: Think about how we put tense endings on verbs when most of the time we also say "yesterday," "last night," and so on.) What does the following sentence mean? Who is doing what to whom?

A la chica la busca el chico.

Right. The boy is looking for the girl.

Actividad G. Select the English rendition of each sentence.

1. *A mi mamá la besa mucho mi papá.*
    a. My mother kisses my dad a lot.
    b. My father kisses my mom a lot.

2. *A mi papá no lo comprendo yo.*
    a. I don't understand my father.
    b. My father doesn't understand me.

3. *A la señora la saluda el señor.*
    a. The woman greets the man.
    b. The man greets the woman.

4. *A los chicos los sorprende la profesora.*
    a. The professor surprises the boys.
    b. The boys surprise the professor.

Actividad H. You will hear some sentences in Spanish. Select the correct picture for each.

1. ☐ a   ☐ b

2. ☐ a   ☐ b

3. ☐ a   ☐ b

4. ☐ a   ☐ b

(For Actividad H, the instructor should read the following sentences.)

1. *A la mujer no la cree el hombre.*
2. *Al hombre la mujer no lo cree.*
3. *Al chico lo sigue la chica.*
4. *El chico sigue a la chica.*

Actividad I. *Un talento especial*

Paso 1. Read the following passage to yourself. Then do the questions that follow.

> Mis abuelos maternos son mexicanos y los quiero mucho. Viven en San José y cuando viajo a California, siempre los visito.
>
> Mi abuela se llama Concepción y es una persona muy especial. Tiene una habilidad psíquica (puede <<ver>> eventos del futuro y del pasado) pero no la usa con mucha frecuencia. Dice que es un regalo de Dios y debe usarla con cuidado (care). Todos en la familia la admiramos mucho.
>
> Una vez la policía la llamó para pedirle ayuda con un crimen (un asesinato). Mi abuela tocó un objeto personal de la víctima y tuvo una <<visión>> del homicidio. Vio muy claro al asesino (sus ojos, color de pelo, etc.) y pronto la policía lo capturó. Mi abuela se convirtió en una celebridad de noche a la mañana (overnight).

Paso 2. Select the title that best fits the passage.

a. <<Mi abuela: víctima de un crimen>>
b. <<Por qué capturaron a mi abuela>>
c. <<Un talento especial>>

Paso 3. Select the best response based on what you read in the passage.

1. *Mi abuela es una celebridad porque...*
   a. *la policía la investigó.*
   b. *un hombre la atacó pero ella pudo desarmarlo.*
   c. *ayudó a la policía.*

2. *Respeto de su poder psíquico...*
   a. *lo usa poco.*
   b. *no lo controla muy bien.*
   c. *no lo toma en serio.*

3. *¿Qué describe mejor mis sentimientos hacia mi abuela?*
   a. *La critico por su locura* (craziness).
   b. *La quiero y la estimo mucho.*
   c. *No tengo reacción porque nunca la veo ni la visito.*

Paso 4. Find the seven third person object pronouns that occur in the passage and underline them. Then tell to what they refer. The first is done for you.

1. ...los *quiero mucho.*   "los" refers to *mis abuelos*
2. _____   _____
3. _____   _____
4. _____   _____
5. _____   _____
6. _____   _____
7. _____   _____

COMPARISON WITH OTHER APPROACHES

The purpose of the present section is to make explicit the similarities and differences between processing instruction and several other approaches. We will make three explicit comparisons: one with general comprehension-based approaches; another with Sharwood Smith's "input enhancement;" and a third with Rutherford's "consciousness raising."

Comprehension-based Approaches

Some scholars of language teaching and many instructors might conclude that processing instruction is another type of comprehension-based instruction. Because learners do not produce targeted grammatical items during structured input activities, and indeed because the term "input" itself suggests comprehension, the conclusion seems logical. However, there is a problem in lumping processing instruction together with comprehension-based approaches to language instruction.

The term "comprehension-based" refers to the general provision of comprehensible input by instructors and materials during the entire course of classroom acquisition. Instructors use the second language as much as possible, modifying it for comprehensibility, and encouraging learners to talk in the second language only when ready. Krashen (1982) has the following to say about language classrooms that sums up the underlying position of most comprehension-based approaches:

> Quite simply, the role of the second or foreign language classroom is to bring a student to a point where he can begin to use the outside world for further second language acquisition. As expressed in Chapter II this means we have to provide students with enough comprehensible input to bring their second language competence to the point where they can begin to understand language leard "on the outside," read, and participate in coversations. Since they will be less than fully competent, we also need to provide them with tools for encouraging and regulatiing input (pp. 160–161).

What Krashen means is that the provision of comprehensible input should be the *sine qua non* of language teaching; other aspects of instruction are peripheral or only useful if they help to make input comprehensible. To be sure, comprehension-based approaches to instruction may vary in the way in which instructors provide comprehensible input to classroom learners and in the quality of the input. Total Physical Response (TPR) makes heavy use of commands as instructors "order" students to perform actions. The Natural Approach uses some TPR techniques but also relies heavily on teacher-talk. Instructors use visuals and objects around which they weave an oral text, involving students in the co-construction of the discourse with simple answers. Content-based instruction is often comprehension-based as well, particularly with low-level learners. In these types of classrooms, instructors teach about subject matter (geography, history, science, etc.) using only the second language. Instructors modify the speech of their "lectures" and "discussions" to make the language comprehensible to their second language audience. Since the focus is on content, like their first language counterparts these instructors make use of slides, pictures, graphs, objects, on-hands experimentation, and other visual aids that assist learners in comprehending the language.

In addition to the presence of input, what is common to all these approaches is that as long as learners show evidence of understanding (comprehension), then acquisition is assumed to proceed. Indeed, Krashen (1982) states this when he says that as long as the affective filter is low, comprehensible input causes acquisition (pp. 20–32). This means that little or no attention should be paid to formal elements of the language by the instructors during classtime or in the evaluation of student performance. The foci of comprehension-based instruction are subsequently reflected in testing; content-based instructors test for content; Natural Approach instructors test for vocabulary, comprehension, and once beyond the earliest stages, for the expression of meaning. (For more detailed information on comprehension-based approaches to language instruction, the reader is referred to Krashen & Terrell, 1983; Richards & Rodgers, 1986; Winitz, 1981).

Although it is true that processing instruction is input-based, it is not equivalent to comprehension-based approaches. This is evident in that processing instruction's point of departure is to get learners to process more form in the input (or to process it correctly). Recall the guidelines for structured input activities outlined earlier. Several of them have been established because of erroneous assumptions on the part of teachers-in-training (and some practicing teachers as well). These assumptions involve a simple equation between processing instruction and comprehension; any input activity that "embedded" the target form was seen to be processing instruction. As we saw, this is not the case. Processing instruction is guided by the insights from theory and research on input processing and attempts to influence input processing itself. Comprehension-based instruction makes no such attempt. Its purpose is to provide comprehensible input to language learners and has not considered what learners do to the input when they "comprehend" it. Whereas comprehension-based approaches ignore the psyholinguistics of intake derivation, processing instruction actively seeks to influence intake derivation.

The point here is that processing instruction is not just another kind of comprehension-based approach to language instruction. *Processing instruction is a specific approach to explicit grammar instruction* and thus falls more clearly within the category of instructional treatments called "focus on form." It is certainly more congruent with comprehension-based approaches to language teaching than the traditional approaches to grammar instruction that we have briefly reviewed, but to equate it with comprehension-based approaches is to ignore its intent and the theory and research that informs it.

Input Enhancement

Sharwood Smith (1993, and elsewhere) has coined the term "input enhancement" to discuss focus on form. In his framework, input enhancement is any external attempt (by instructors or materials) to make features of the input more salient to learners and could come in many forms. He has discussed both positive and negative enhancement (Sharwood Smith, 1993, p. 177). Positive enhancement could be as simple as color coding or boldfacing forms in reading texts. Negative enhancement involves providing learners with information that a given form is incorrect (e.g., pointing out an error, making a funny face, or offering a quizzical look when an error is produced).

Processing instruction is consonant with Sharwood Smith's position but also goes beyond it in an important way. Note that Sharwood Smith is concerned with making forms salient, that is, bringing them to learners attention in some way. Processing instruction does this but also attempts to provide opportunities for consistent form-meaning mappings in activities. Simply bringing a form to someone's attention is no guarantee that it gets processed at all or gets processed correctly (see Chapter 2). For acquisition to happen, the intake must continually provide the developing system with examples of correct form-meaning connections that are the result of input processing.

In addition, processing instruction makes no claims about providing so-called negative enhancement regarding learners' errors. Since it is solely concerned with the processing of input data, explanation and practice are completely input-based. It is true that processing instruction is concerned with erroneous input processing and attempts to circumvent it; however, processing instruction does not address the role of output errors in second language development.

Consciousness Raising

Rutherford (1987, and elsewhere) has discussed "grammatical consciousness raising," which is, simply put, any "deliberate attempt to draw the learner's attention specifically to the formal properties of the target language" (Rutherford & Sharwood Smith, 1988, p. 107). What Rutherford says is that language acquisition can be aided by such consciousness raising, but that the actual form of consciousness raising can vary depending on first-second language contrasts and the nature of the grammatical item or structure. Although the exact content and nature of consciousness raising is amorphous, one thing is clear; for Rutherford, consciousness raising cannot be equated with traditional grammar instruction. The latter, according to Rutherford, is an attempt to instill grammatical form in the learner, equivalent to writing upon the proverbial tabula rasa. Consciousness raising, on the other hand, does not instill anything; instead it assists the processes that underly acquisition of grammar and does not presume to contain the knowledge (or product) that must eventually be acquired (Rutherford, 1987, 24).

In a real sense, processing instruction is a type of consciousness raising, although the term "consciousness" is somewhat unfortunate. Since processing instruction attempts to influence the processes involved in the derivation of intake, it is not a product-oriented approach to grammar teaching that Rutherford appears to critique. That is, processing instruction does not seek to "pour knowledge" of any kind into learners' heads; it assists certain processes that can aid the growth of the developing system over time. For this reason, we conclude that Rutherford would not have much problem in considering processing instruction as one manifestation of grammatical consciousness raising.

As noted earlier, the term consciousness is somewhat unfortunate. The term carries with it the idea in many individual's beliefs that conscious (explicit) knowledge must precede subconscious (implicit) knowledge, something that Rutherford surely would not prescribe. Thus, a justification for consciousness raising might lead these readers to justify traditional grammar instruction if they do not grasp Rutherford's major distinctions (see the preceding discussion). As a probable type of consciousness raising, processing instruction does not claim that explicit knowledge leads to implicit knowledge and does not prescribe any role for explicit knowledge. Indeed we cannot know what kind of grammatical knowledge is contained in the developing system. Again, at the risk of being repetitive, we state here that processing instruction is concerned with delivering form-meaning connections as intake to the developing system. The ways in which the developing system accommodates these data and eventually restructures is beyond the scope of both input processing and processing instruction. Thus, whatever so-called explicit or conscious knowledge is contained in processing instruction (i.e., the explanation part of processing instruction) is not what exists in the developing system that is tapped for output processing. We would prefer, then, to think of our approach to instruction as not about raising learners' consciousness about grammatical form but instead as enriching their subconscious intake.

CONCLUSION

We have described processing instruction in some detail in this chapter, focusing on the nature of structured input activities. We have seen that processing instruction is not just explanation about language and grammatical form. It includes information to the learner about what to attend to in the input. Most importantly, it includes structured input activities that encourage learners to make form-meaning mappings they might not make when exposed to nonstructured or "spontaneous" input. An important aspect of structured input activities is that learners attend to the meaning of an input sentence. It is not enough that learners simply be directed to the form; they must also use it to comprehend the meaning of the sentence. Thus, the activities are formulated with the processing strategies of learners in mind.

A number of issues arise from the presentation in this chapter. Since input processing here is related to form-meaning mappings, is it possible to use processing instruction for forms that do not carry meaning? A related issue is the relationship of processing instruction and input processing to the acquisition of syntactic rules. Many syntactic rules do not seem to be motivated by meaning and at first glance it does appear that processing instruction is useful in terms of helping learners acquire these rules. These are important issues and we will address them in Chapter 5. First, however, we will examine the research that supports the effectiveness of processing instruction.

4

RESEARCH ON PROCESSING INSTRUCTION

INTRODUCTION

Suggestions about second language classroom methodology come and go. Richards and Rodgers (1986) and Larsen-Freeman (1986), for example, examine methodologies such as Suggestopedia, The Natural Approach, Total Physical Response, The Silent Way, Community Counselling Learning, among others. What is interesting about these methodological innovations is that their purported benefits are seldom researched. Empirical studies about what learners gain in such programs as opposed to others just can't be found in the literature on second language learning and teaching. Only the outcomes of immersion approaches in Canada seem to be investigated with any consistency (e.g., Harley and Swain, 1984; Swain, 1985).

Research on explicit grammar instruction and focus on form, however, is much more plentiful as evidenced in reviews such as Chapter 8 of Larsen-Freeman and Long (1991), Chapter 14 of Ellis (1994), and Chapter 5 of Lightbown and Spada (1993). This plentifulness may be owing to the rather narrow focus of the research; research on grammar instruction and focus on form examines only one of the many components of any given methodology and thus the research is easier to conduct than research that examines a method in its entirety. The plentifulness may be owing to innovations in theory about language or innovations in research methodology that suggest new research paradigms. Or, the plentifulness of the research may be owing to the fact that grammar instruction and focus on form have been hotly debated topics in second language studies for some time. People are simply interested in the issues related to these topics and they just don't go away.

The purpose of the present chapter is to examine the empirical studies that have been conducted on processing instruction. Because it is a type of focus on form and not a methodology, processing instruction is readily researchable and to date five major studies have been conducted on it. All five studies involve the learning of Spanish, although there is research in progress that includes learners of English. The first study that we will review is VanPatten and Cadierno (1993). This was the first empirical investigation on processing instruction and its benefits. Since the study focused on object pronouns and word order, we classify it here as a study about the acquisition of syntax. The second study, by Cadierno (1995), focuses on the past tense, whereas the third, VanPatten and Sanz (1995), is a partial replication of VanPatten and Cadierno and examines whether or not the effects of processing instruction are observable in a variety of meaning-based and communicative tasks. The fourth study, by Cheng (1995), focuses on the acquisition of lexical-aspectual items, namely, the copular verbs in Spanish. In short, we have three empirical studies reporting on different types of grammatical features in Spanish and one study that focuses on the assessment tasks used in research on processing instruction. The fifth and final study, VanPatten and Oikkenon (1996), reports on the role of explicit information in processing instruction.

RESEARCH ON SYNTAX:
OBJECT PRONOUNS AND WORD ORDER IN SPANISH

Overview

VanPatten and Cadierno (1993) set out to investigate processing instruction based on P3, the first noun strategy, with learners of Spanish. Because the research methodology they used influenced subsequent studies, we will spend considerable time describing and reviewing it here. Their research questions were the following:

1. Does altering the way in which learners process input have an effect on their developing systems?
2. If there is an effect, is it limited solely to processing more input or does instruction in input processing also have an effect on output?
3. If there is an effect, is it the same effect that traditional instruction has (assuming an effect for the latter)?

Motivation for the Study

As we saw in Chapter 2, second language learners are known to assign the first noun of an input sentence the role of subject even if it is something else, reflecting some universal principles of semantic role assignment. VanPatten

(1984b) shows that learners consistently misinterpret sentences such as *La visita el chico* as "She visits the boy" rather than the correct "The boy visits her." LoCoco (1987) has demonstrated that learners misinterpret sentences such as *Hacia la madre empuja el chico a su padre* as "The mother pushes the boy to the father" rather than the correct "The boy pushes his father toward his mother." (For additional research, see Binkowski, 1992; Gass, 1989; Lee, 1987.) VanPatten and Cadierno argued that this processing strategy may cause learners of Spanish a number of problems in delivering intake to the developing system. First, it may cause learners to misinterpret object pronouns as subjects if the subject is null or post-posed after the verb (see the preceding example). Alternatively, if the subject *is* present and is also preverbal, learners may not attend to the object pronoun once they assign the subject its grammatical and semantic role. Learners might simply "fill-in" the object based on lexical semantics and context, not relying on the grammatical cue in the input sentence. Another problem is that learners may skip over the object marker *a* in the input. If they are relying on word order, then the object marker is of relatively low communicative value for processing the meaning of the sentence. Finally, learners may not rely on verb endings as cues to the subject when the subject and object are of differing number (i.e., one plural and the other singular). Given P1(b), that learners will process lexical items before grammatical items that encode the same semantic information, learners may simply not process verb endings if the subject is present or if they misassign the object pronoun the grammatical role of subject. The result of these possibilities is incorrect intake data delivered to the developing system as evidenced by a number of learner errors: (1) misuse of object and reflexive pronouns for subjects, for example, *Lo viene* for "He comes," *Me hablo* for "I talk;" (2) problems with *gustar*, for example, *Yo gusto mi profesor* for "I like my professor;" (3) a general over-reliance on subject pronouns (e.g., *Manuel es mi compañero de cuarto. Lo es muy simpático. Él estudia arte.*"); (4) a complete lack of use of the direct object case marker *a*, for example, *Yo no llamo mis padres*; (5) an overreliance on subject-verb-object word order and problems in the acquisition of object pronouns, for example, *Ellos llama mi*, and (6) a delay in the acquisition of person-number endings. In short, this one processing strategy may have a significant effect on a number of areas of the learner's developing system of Spanish.

Subjects and Groups

VanPatten and Cadierno used the first noun strategy as the starting point for their study. They compared three groups of learners in the acquisition of object pronouns: (1) a control group that received no instruction: (2) a traditional group that received instruction based on one of the most widely adopted college-level textbooks and its accompanying workbook and lab manual; and (3) a processing group that received instruction developed by VanPatten and subsequently incorporated into VanPatten, Lee, Glass, and Binkowski (1992).

Six second-year classes of Spanish from the University of Illinois were randomly assigned to one of the three treatment groups, whole classes being used to avoid problems inherent in voluntary self-selection of subjects. After pretesting and screening of subjects for a variety of background variables including first language, previous study of Spanish, knowledge of other Romance languages, and hearing and learning impairments, a total of 80 subjects participated in all phases of the study: 27 in the control group; 26 in the traditional group; and 27 in the processing group. Subjects were students in a language program with a communicative methodology based on the Natural Approach. Grammar instruction was absent from class time, although subjects routinely completed some grammar focused exercises outside of class as homework. Classes met four days a week with the majority of class time spent on interaction, listening, and reading. At no time during the course of the study were object pronouns or word order a focus of study in the subjects' homework. All subjects' first language was English.

Instruction and Treatment Materials

Instruction for both the traditional and processing groups consisted of two days of class time with no outside homework; in each group the teaching materials were picked up at the end of the first class day as well as at the end of the second class day. Two days are about the normal amount of time that a language curriculum in Spanish would devote to the explicit learning of object pronouns. At no time were the subjects or their regular instructors aware that this was a comparative study and that learners in other classes were receiving different instruction.

The traditional materials consisted of explanation and exercises taken largely from *Puntos de partida* and its accompanying workbook and lab manual. The researchers chose this textbook because at the time of the study it was the most widely sold and used college-level textbook in Spanish and probably represented typical grammar instruction for most college-level instructors. In these materials, students receive the full paradigm of direct object pronouns in Spanish, an explanation of what direct object pronouns are and where they are placed in a sentence. Students are subsequently led through a number of oral mechanical practices, oral meaningful practices, and finally oral communicative practices. (See the description of Paulston's hierarchy in Chapter 1 of the present book.) The workbook and laboratory materials consist largely of mechanical and meaningful oral and written practices. Emphasis is always on production albeit manipluated production.

Processing instruction consisted of the explanations and activity types described in detail in Chapter 3. Recall that the emphasis in these materials is on processing input and making correct form-meaning mappings. At no time did the subjects in the processing group produce an object pronoun during the instructional phase.

As they developed the materials, VanPatten and Cadierno made adjustments in activities in order to balance the two sets of teaching materials and control for possible features that might influence the outcome of the study. Specifically, VanPatten and Cadierno controlled for the following features: total number of activities, total number of tokens (sentences produced in the traditional group versus sentences interpreted in the processing group), percentage of whole-class activities versus percentage of pair activities, percentage of oral (aural) versus written activities, and number of visuals. In addition, VanPatten and Cadierno altered vocabulary in the activities so that the vocabulary used in each packet was roughly the same and consisted of highly frequent and familiar vocabulary for students of second-year Spanish. At the same time, VanPatten and Cadierno checked the vocabulary in the instructional packets against the vocabulary used in the assessment tasks in order to avoid a vocabulary bias for one group or the other.

Since VanPatten and Cadierno were interested in the relative benefits of two different kinds of focus on form, they also controlled for a factor known to affect similar studies: the instructor. Previous comparison research has shown that instructors may bias toward one approach or another and affect the outcomes of research (see, e.g., Spada & Lightbown, 1993). Rather than allow the regular classroom instructors to deliver the treatment, VanPatten and Cadierno removed these instructors during the treatment and testing periods. Instead, Cadierno taught both experimental groups. Experienced in traditional instruction but not in processing instruction, she very carefully adhered to the tenets of the two approaches and made sure that at no time during processing instruction did the subjects produce utterances with object pronouns. Cadierno's hypotheses at the outset of the treatment period were that the traditional group would be better at producing object pronouns and that the processing group would be better at comprehending them. She kept these hypotheses until the first round of results appeared and as we will see, her own hypotheses and past experience in teaching with traditional instruction did not influence the outcome of the study.

Pre- and Posttests

A pretest/posttest design was used to measure gains due to instruction. Four versions (A, B, C, and D) of two different assessment tasks were developed. The first was an interpretation task. In this task, learners heard 10 target sentences along with five distractors. Five target sentences were of the order object pronoun-verb-subject and the other five were of the order object marker + noun-object pronoun-verb-subject. The five distractors were subject-verb-object sentences. All sentences were simple declarative sentences in the present-tense containing familiar vocabulary. Subjects demonstrated interpretation of each sentence by selecting one of two drawings projected on an overhead screen in front of the class. Thus, for the sentence *A la chica la abraza la mamá* "The mother hugs the girl," subjects chose between a picture of a woman hugging a child (who does not hug back) and a picture of a child hugging a woman (who does not hug back). This task had a time limit. Once the subjects heard a sentence, they had eight seconds to make their picture selection before the pictures were removed and they heard the next sentence.

The second assessment task was a sentence-level written production task consisting of five target items. Each item consisted of a two-part sentence that corresponded to a two-part drawing. The second part of each sentence was incomplete and was to be completed by the subject based on the visual cues. For example, one item was *El chico piensa en la chica y entonces* _____ "The boy is thinking about the girl and so _____." The two-frame picture that accompanied this sentence shows the boy thinking about the girl in frame one and then calling her in frame two. The correct expected response would be to write *y entonces la llama* "and so he calls her." All sentences were simple declarative sentences in the present-tense containing familiar vocabulary. This task also had a time limit. Subjects had 15 seconds to complete each sentence after they saw the pictures. (Time limits and vocabulary familiarity were determined by pilot testing of both the interpretation and production tasks.)

In order to break up the presentation of the two assessment tasks, VanPatten and Cadierno administered a 10-minute distractor task between the interpretation and production tasks. This distractor task consisted of 10 sentences to be translated from Spanish to English with none containing object pronouns.

We should point out here that the two assessment tasks used by VanPatten and Cadierno were designed purposefully to counter test bias. Note that the interpretation task would favor the processing group since it is similar to if not identical to some of the treatment activities used in processing instruction (see Chapter 3). At the same time, the production task would favor the traditional group. The design for this particular task was identical to several of the production tasks included in the treatment materials for the traditional group. Thus, VanPatten and Cadierno were able, if necessary, to account for any apparent task biases should they appear in the results. As we will see, however, this was not the case.

Scoring

Each target item in the interpretation task received a score of 1 or 0, 1 for correct picture selection and 0 for incorrect selection or nonselection. The total points possible was 10.

Each target item in the production task received a score of 2, 1, or 0 points. If the subject produced a correct object pronoun and also placed it in the correct position in the sentence the item received a score of 2. If the subject failed to produce any object pronoun even if the sentence was correct by any other standard, the item received a score of 0. Inbetween cases (correct object pronoun produced but in the wrong place, incorrect object pronoun used but in the correct place, incorrect object pronoun in an incorrect position) received a score of 1. VanPatten and Cadierno adopted this liberal scoring procedure for inbetween cases in the event that the instructional treatments had some effect but subjects had yet to fully internalized the target linguistic feature. Note, however, that in cases in which it was clear that the research subject was using the object pronoun as a subject pronoun, the researchers assigned the score of 0, e.g., *y entonces lo llama a la chica* in which *lo* is incorrectly used for subject "he" and not object "him."

The pretest versions of the tests were used to establish baseline data and to eliminate subjects from the pool. VanPatten and Cadierno established an arbitrary 80% ceiling on the pretest for admission into the study; subjects who scored 80% and above on the pretest were eliminated since they were already performing at levels in which they might not be affected by instruction and could possibly skew the data. The group sizes given in the section above on subjects are the final group sizes after pretesting.

Summary of Research Design

The research design in VanPatten and Cadierno, then, can be summarized in Figure 4-1. We add here that all testing and instruction was conducted in the subjects' regular classrooms and that the three posttests were administered immediately after the treatment on the second day of instruction, two weeks later, and one month later. The four versions of the tests (A, B, C, and D—see earlier on pre- and posttests), were used to create a split-block design to control for test order. Thus, one group might receive test A first and then B, C, and D as the three posttests, whereas another might receive B as the pre-test with D, C, and A as the three posttests, and so on. Raw scores were submitted to two separate one-way analyses of variance (ANOVA) with a repeated measures design. One of the ANOVAs was conducted using the scores of the intepretation task, whereas the other was conducted based on the scores of the production task. Instruction was the label used for the three treament groups, whereas time was the label used for the pre- and two posttests.

Results

An ANOVA on both intererpretation and production pretests revealved no significant differences between the three groups prior to instruction. Thus, results obtained on posttest measures are attributable to instructional effects.

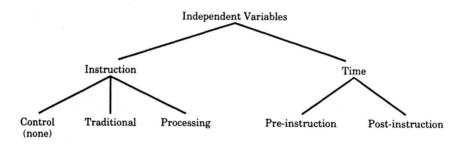

Dependent variables = scores on interpretation and
production tasks

FIGURE 4-1. Research design in VanPatten and Cadierno (1993).

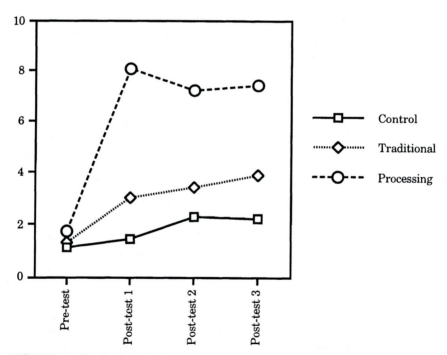

FIGURE 4-2. Results from VanPatten and Cadierno (1993) on the interpretation task.

The results from VanPatten and Cadierno's study are interesting. On the intepretation task, there was a main effect for instruction, a main effect for time, and a significant interaction between instruction and time. Post-hoc tests revealed that the main effect for instruction was owing to the following:

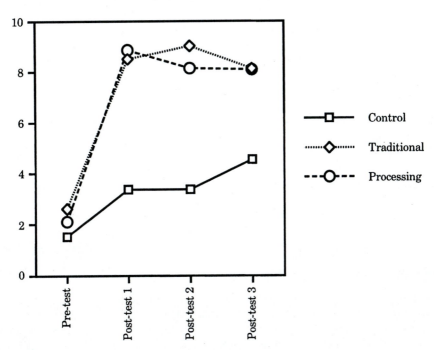

FIGURE 4-3. Results from VanPatten and Cadierno (1993) on the production task.

Table 4-1. ANOVA Summaries for both Interpretation and Production Tasks in VanPatten and Cadierno (1993)

	df	SS	MS	F-value
Interpretation task				
Source of variation				
Instruction	2	1094.646	547.323	33.129**
Time	3	521.531	173.844	76.921**
Time × instruction	6	297.150	49.525	21.913**
Production task				
Source of variation				
Instruction	2	991.937	495.969	25.214**
Time	3	1361.453	453.818	97.016**
Time × instruction	6	244.392	40.732	8.708**

**p < .01.

the processing group made significant gains, whereas the traditional and control groups did not. The main effect for time was due to the following: The posttest scores were significantly greater than the pre-test scores. The interaction was owing to the fact that the post-test scores for the processing group were greater than its pretest scores, but this was not true for the control and traditional groups. These findings are summarized in Figure 4-2, which gives a sense of the tremendous gains made by the processing group.

The results on the production task were the same as for the interpretation task, but for a different reason. The ANOVA yielded a main effect for instruction, for time, and a significant interaction between time and instruction. However, the post-hoc tests revealed that the effect for instruction was due to the fact that both the processing and traditional groups showed gains, whereas the control group did not. In addition, the processing and traditional groups posttest scores were not significantly different from each other. The effect for time again was due to the pre-test/post-test differences, and the interaction between time and instruction was due to the two treatment groups' post-test scores being significantly higher than those of the control group. Figure 4-3 summarizes these findings.

Table 4-1 displays the actual results of the two Analyses of Variance for those who wish to see the actual F and p values.

Discussion of the Findings

The results from VanPatten and Cadierno's study suggest that processing instruction is more beneficial than traditional instruction. Subjects in this group not only gained in ability to interpret word order and object pronouns correctly, but apparently the intake data made available to the developing system as a result of input processing had an impact on the system such that learners were able to access the new knowledge and use it during production. This is significant since *at no time did the subjects in the processing group engage in production activities during instruction*. At the same time, the traditional group made gains only in production and not in interpretation, suggesting that intruction did not affect their developing system (a point we will explore in the next chapter). Thus the answers to VanPatten and Cadierno's research questions are: (1) yes, altering the way in which learners process input data does have an effect on their developing systems; (2) the effect is not limited to input processing but is also observable in output; (3) processing and traditional instruction have differential effects, with processing instruction being superior overall.

There are two limitations to the VanPatten and Cadierno study that merit attention here. One is that the assessment tasks used were highly controlled sentence-level tasks. Although VanPatten and Cadierno were not researching effects across different tasks but relative effects on one task attributable to different instructional treatments, this limitation is important since we would like to know whether or not learners can access their systems on less controlled and more communicative tasks. We will take this up in a later section of this chapter when we review VanPatten and Sanz (1995). The other limitation is that only one aspect of input processing was investigated, P3, the first noun strategy. What of the other principles of input processing outlined in Chapter 2 and the effects that they have on acquisition? We turn our attention now to a study on verb inflections.

RESEARCH ON VERB INFLECTIONS: THE SPANISH PAST-TENSE

Overview

Cadierno (1995) reported on a study in which she investigated the benefits of both traditional and processing instruction on the acquisition of the preterit tense (simple past) in Spanish. Her study was based on P1(b), that learners process lexical items as opposed to grammatical form when both encode the same semantic information. Cadierno posed the following research questions at the outset of her study:

1. Will there be any difference in how learners receiving no instruction, processing instruction, and traditional instruction interpret sentences in which past temporal reference is only expressed by verb morphology?
2. Will there be any differences in how learners receiving no instruction, processing instruction, and traditional instruction produce correct past tense forms to express past tense meanings?

Motivation for the Study

The preterit tense is a morphologically complex system for learners of Spanish. Unlike English, there are some 16 different forms for the regular preterit tense owing to the inflections for both tense and person-number and the type of verb being inflected. Also unlike English, the Spanish preterit undergoes a stress shift from the stem of the verb to the actual tense inflection with the exception of first person and second person plural. In addition, various classes of verbs undergo a stem-vowel alternation in certain forms of the preterit. This past tense system is compounded by the presence of a highly frequent irregular subsystem in which the stress shift does not occur and in which the stems of verbs undergo both vowel and final consonant alterations. The preterit system is notoriously difficult for learners of Spanish.

Cadierno reasoned that one of the problems in the acquisition of the preterit system in Spanish is that learners may not attend to the verbal inflections in the input. Citing P1(b), which she calls "the lexical processing strategy," Cadierno suggested that learners rely on lexical items such as adverbials of temporal reference to interpret the tense of a sentence and ignore the verbal inflections. (See Chapter 2 for details on P1(b) and a review of the relevant research.) She thus concluded that processing instruction, in which the adverbials of temporal reference were removed from the structured input sentences, would push learners to attend to the connection between tense and verb endings. Learners would use the verbal inflections as indicators of tense since the lexical indicators of tense would be absent.

The Study

Given that Cadierno's study on the preterit tense was an almost exact replication of VanPatten and Cadierno (1993) reviewed in the previous section, we will not examine the specifics of her study in as much detail as we did for VanPatten and Cadierno. We will instead make references to VanPatten and Cadierno as we proceed, noting differences between the two studies as appropriate.

Subjects and Groups

Cadierno compared three groups: a control group ($n=20$), a group receiving traditional instruction ($n=19$), and a group receiving processing instruction ($n=22$). The subjects came from the same population as that described in VanPatten and Cadierno but were not the same subjects. Cadierno screened her subjects for background as in VanPatten and Cadierno and also used a 60% cutoff score on pretests (more stringent than in the VanPatten and Cadierno study) to ensure a more homogenous pool of subjects. Only subjects who completed all phases of the experiment remained in the final subject pool. The n sizes given above were the final n sizes. Subjects in all three groups were unaware of the comparative nature of the study.

Instructional Treatment

As in the VanPatten and Cadierno study, Cadierno developed a set of teaching materials for the traditional group based on *Puntos de partida*. She also developed a set of materials for processing instruction and then balanced the two sets of materials for those potential intervening features mentioned previously: number of tokens, activity types, use of visuals, vocabulary, and so on. Processing instruction here focused on removing temporal adverbs from the structured input activities so that learner attention could be directed toward verb endings as indicators of tense. Instruction for both treatment groups consisted of a two-day treatment in class with no outside homework.

The control group continued with their regular activities and at no time during the experimental treatment were the subjects of any group scheduled to receive instruction on the past tense as part of the regular coursework. The regular classroom instructors were removed during all testing and treatment periods with the researcher conducting all testing and instruction herself.

Assessment Tasks and Scoring

Cadierno developed four versions (A, B, C, and D) of two assessment tasks, an interpretation task and and production task. The interpretation task was a 20-item aural test of simple sentences *without adverbial indications of temporal reference*, e.g., *Antonio llamó a sus padres por teléfono,* "Anthony called his parents on the phone." Of these sentences, 10 items were in the present tense (distractors) and 10 items in the past tense (target items). Subjects had to listen to the sentence and then indicate whether the sentence they heard was in the present or past tense or whether they could not tell. The production task consisted of five written items with blanks in which the learner had to complete the sentence with a correct verb cued by an infinitive in parentheses, e.g., *Ayer yo* _____ *(escuchar) las noticias,* "Yesterday I _____ (listen) to the news." Cadierno imposed time limits for both tasks as described for VanPatten and Cadierno. She also administered an intervening distractor task consisting of translation sentences unrelated to tense distinction.

Following VanPatten and Cadierno, Cadierno utilized a split block design and administered one pre-test and three post-tests varying the test versions among the groups. The post-tests were administered immediately after instruction, two weeks later, and one month later.

Scoring for the interpretation task consisted of a 1 versus 0 point system per item for a total possible of 10 points. A subject received 1 point if the target sentence was assigned correctly past tense reference and received 0 points if the tense assignment was wrong or the subject indicated an inability to determine the tense. Cadierno scored the production task using a 2, 1, 0 point system for a possible total of 10 points. A subject received 2 points if the sentence completion contained a verb in the correct preterit form. If the verb was in the past tense but was the wrong person or if the verb was in the past tense but the subject had switched verb category endings, the subject received a score of 1. Any other response received a score of 0.

Results

Cadierno conducted separate one-way ANOVAs on each assessment task using raw scores as the dependent variable. She used instruction (the various treatment groups) and time (pre- vs. posttests) as the labels for the independent variables. A preliminary set of ANOVAs on the pretest scores

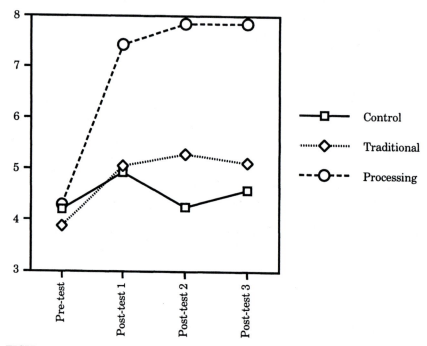

FIGURE 4-4. Results from Cadierno (1995) on the interpretation task.

revealed no significant differences between the three groups prior to the instructional treatments. Once again, any observable effects are attributed to the instructional treatments.

Cadierno's results were identical to those of VanPatten and Cadierno. For the interpretation task, she found a main effect for instruction, a main effect for time, and a significant interaction between instruction and time. Once again the post hoc tests revealed that the effects were due to the following contrasts: The processing group improved significantly from pre- to posttests, whereas the traditional and control groups did not. In addition, there was no significant difference between the control and traditional groups. These findings are displayed graphically in Figure 4-4.

For the production task, the ANOVA yielded a main effect for instruction, a main effect for time, and a significant interaction between instruction and time. As with the results of VanPatten and Cadierno, these effects were caused by the following contrasts as revealed through post hoc tests: Both the traditional and the processing group improved significantly, whereas the control group did not. There was no difference between the performance of the traditional and processing groups. The results of the production task are displayed in Figure 4-5.

Once again, for those who wish to see the F and p values of the analyses, these are presented in Table 4-2.

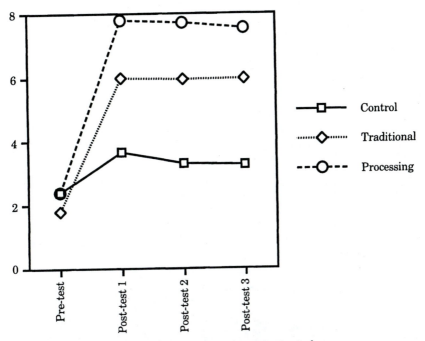

FIGURE 4-5. Results from Cadierno (1995) on the production task.

Table 4-2. ANOVA Summaries for both Interpretation and Production Tasks in Cadierno (1995)

	df	SS	MS	F-value
Interpretation task				
Source of variation				
Instruction	2	228.980	114.490	27.379**
Time	3	115.561	38.250	23.238**
Time × instruction	6	80.730	13.455	8.117**
Production task				
Source of variation				
Instruction	2	394.624	197.312	11.526**
Time	3	508.399	169.466	58.442**
Time × instruction	6	141.203	23.534	8.116**

**p < .01.

Discussion of the Findings

Cadierno's findings on the acquisition of the past tense support the findings and conclusions reported in VanPatten and Cadierno; processing instruction seems to be more beneficial than traditional instruction. Subjects receiving processing instruction make gains in both the ability to assign tense to input sentences when adverbials are absent and in the ability to produce past tense forms. Subjects receiving traditional instruction make gains only in production of past tense forms. The answers to Cadierno's research questions, then, are: (1) there is a difference in the way in which the three groups interpret past tense sentences in which tense is encoded solely in the verb morphology; only processing instruction improves the learner's ability to do this; (2) there is no difference in the way that learners receiving processing instruction and traditional instruction produce verb forms after treatment; both result in improved performance. Again we point out that the findings are especially remarkable considering that the subjects in the processing group never once produced past tense forms during the instructional treatment.

We thus have evidence so far that processing instruction is indeed beneficial for learners and is superior to traditional instruction. The evidence is based on two distinct target linguistic items, one syntactic the other morphological. To be sure, Cadierno's research suffers from the same major limitation as that of VanPatten and Cadierno's, that we have no evidence that the benefits of processing instruction are available during more communicative tasks. We turn our attention now to this issue.

RESEARCH ON COMMUNICATIVE OUTPUT: SENTENCE-LEVEL VERSUS DISCOURSE-LEVEL TASKS

Overview

In their discussion of their results, VanPatten and Cadierno (1993, pp. 238–239) recognize that their results do not address the issue of ability to use grammar in communicative performance. Since their aim was to compare the relative effects of processing and traditional instruction, they did not see the need to incorporate a battery of tasks to measure whether or not instruction results in more accurate performance during communicative tasks.

VanPatten and Sanz (1995) set out to research this limitation in both the VanPatten and Cadierno and the Cadierno studies. In a partial replication of VanPatten and Cadierno's study utilizing only a control group and a processing group, they compared the effects of instruction on three output measures: (1) the same sentence-level task as used in VanPatten & Cadierno; (2) a structured question-answer interview; and (3) a video narration task. The basic research question they asked is the following:

1. Do the observed effects for processing instruction on the sentence level task also obtain on other language production tasks?

Since both the VanPatten and Cadierno study and the Cadierno study utilized written production tasks, VanPatten and Sanz also wanted to know whether oral versus written production were equally or differentially affected by processing instruction. Thus a secondary question is the following:

2. Assuming the effects for processing instruction are observable in all three assessment tasks, does the mode of task (written vs. oral) make a difference?

Motivation for the Study

An examination of the production tasks used in the previously reviewed studies on processing instruction reveal that the tasks are essentially sentence-level tasks. Although a time limit was imposed for the completion of each item, it could be argued that the tasks invite monitoring since they appear to be form focused and quite controlled. In VanPatten and Cadierno, the production task was a sentence completion task in which subjects had to write a short phrase based on a visual cue. In Cadierno, the production task was a fill-in-the-blank task in which subjects only had to provide a verb. In each case, the learners need only focus on the grammar to be used since all lexical material and context was supplied by the stimuli. These tasks have face validity for instructors, since they resemble the grammar testing that many instructors utilize. Thus, anyone who wishes to argue that the testing was unfair to subjects in the traditional groups, cannot make the argument.

However, as pointed out in VanPatten (1988), one of the problems of research on the effects of instruction *in general* is that assessment tasks normally do not measure communicative ability. As knowledge-based tasks, they supply the researcher with information about possible changes in the developing system but they do not supply us with information about communicative performance. These tasks include sentence-level completion as in the VanPatten and Cadierno study, fill-in-the-blanks as in the Cadierno study, as well as sentence combining, grammaticality judgments, error detection, cloze tests, elicited imitation, and other tasks.

Because of these assessment limitations, it is easy to dismiss the observed beneficial results of processing instruction described in the previous studies. VanPatten and Sanz thus decided to investigate the effects of processing instruction independently of the effects of traditional instruction by adding two more assessment tasks that involve language production beyond the sentence level. In this way, they could observe whether or not the mechanisms for making output could make use of the new knowledge in the developing system. Once again, since the study relies largely on VanPatten and Cadierno's research design, we will be brief in our presentation, pointing out the major differences between the two studies as appropriate.

The Study

Subjects and Groups

Subjects were once again students of Spanish at the second-year college-level culled from the same population as the previous studies but were not the same subjects. Since VanPatten and Sanz were concerned with assessment tasks and not traditional versus processing instruction, they utilized only two groups: a control group and a processing group. After background screening, participation in all phases of the study, and performance at 60% or below on the pre-test (see the section that follows, Assessment Tasks and Scoring), their final pool consisted of 44 subjects: 27 in the processing group and 17 in the control group. At no time during the experiment did subjects receive regular instruction on the target items.

Instructional Treatment

Subjects in the processing group received the exact same two-day instructional treatment as the subjects in the VanPatten and Cadierno study. The focus was on object pronouns and word order with the materials designed to alter subjects' reliance on the first noun strategy. The control group received no instruction and continued with its regular classroom activities during the two-day period in which the processing group received its instruction. The regular instructor for the processing group was removed and replaced by Sanz during the treatment period. As in the previous study, subjects in both groups were unaware of research being conducted in the other group.

Assessment Tasks and Scoring

VanPatten and Sanz used a split-block design with various versions of each assessment task and different orders of presentation to control for test bias. Each task was administered twice; once a as a pretest and once as a posttest immediately following instruction. The new tasks were developed by Sanz as part of her dissertation research (Sanz-Alcalá, 1994).

The first task was an interpretation task. The only difference between it and the one used in the VanPatten and Cadierno study was that the number of target items was doubled; the task contained 20 targeted items and 10 distractors. The 1 versus 0 scoring procedure from VanPatten and Cadierno was used once again. Since VanPatten and Sanz were concerned with peformance on various output tasks, the purpose of the interpretation task was to narrow the subject pool. First, it served to eliminate subjects prior to treatment; only subjects who scored 60% or below on the pretest remained in the subject pool. Second, it served as a pretest/posttest measure of effects on the developing system; only processing subjects who showed a gain after treatment remained in the subject pool for the analyses of the output tasks. The reasoning here was that we were testing the effects of processing instruction on output and wanted to see if those who benefited by processing instruction on the interpretation task where no output is required, could subsequently use their new knowledge on output tasks.

VanPatten and Sanz utilized three different production tasks. The first was a sentence-level completion task identical to that used in VanPatten and Cadierno with the exception that 14 sentences were used rather than five: eight target items and six distractors.

The second production task was a question-answer task based on a series of pictures that described a story. The series contained seven pictures and subjects had to answer 11 questions based on what they saw in the pictures. Of these 11 questions, seven were target questions. A sample target question is *¿Qué hace el chico con la banana?* "What is the boy doing with the banana?" These types of questions would require a direct object pronoun and a conjugated verb within a simple sentence in naturally occurring discourse, for example, *La saca de la canasta,* "He is taking it out of the basket."

The third production task consisted of a story telling task in which subjects recounted the events they saw in a brief two-minute video clip. Each video story contained seven connected events. As an example, one clip involved a man who comes home with his groceries, pulls out a potato, washes it, peels it, cuts it up, fries it, and so on, until he eats it. The instructions specified that the subject should provide as much detail as possible, so that a student in another class could identify the video clip being described from among a series of video clips. This was done not only to elicit as much information as possible, but also to provide a communicative context to the task. Each video clip was shown twice and the subjects were required to tell the story only after viewing it the second time. In this way, subjects created a short monologue of connected utterances in which object pronouns should be used to avoid unnatural repetition of object nouns.

Because VanPatten and Sanz were also interested in the effects of oral versus written mode on performance, they created both a written and an oral version of each of the preceding tests. Thus, in the sentence-completion task, subjects had to either respond orally or in writing. In the question-answer task, subjects had to respond in writing to written questions about the pictures or orally to aural questions about the pictures. In the video narration task, subjects either wrote out a narration or they produced an oral narration.

The use of three different production tasks with varying numbers of items and types of responses, created a problem in comparability. To solve this, VanPatten and Sanz first transformed all scored into ratios. To do this, they formed a denominator using the number of of critical items multiplied by two. They then calculated the numerator by adding the amount of correct responses multiplied by two, the amount of incorrect attempts multiplied by one and the amount of cases in which the item was not supplied at all multiplied by 0. Because of the nature of the video narration test, each subject could produce a different number of sentences with preverbal object pronouns, which means that the denominator in the ratio could vary. To account for this, a special procedure was followed. One native speaker read the protocols and decided on the number of obligatory occasions for the use of preverbal object pronouns generated by the subject. The number of occasions was multiplied by two and the result, representing the total possible points, was the denominator of a ratio. Two other native speakers independently scored a sample of the protocols and agreed on 100% of the cases.

After deriving the ratios for all three tasks, VanPatten and Sanz transformed the ratios into percentages and then transformed these percentages via a special function—$y'=2 \arcsin(\sqrt{y})$— in order to satisfy the ANOVA normality assumption.

To summarize, VanPatten and Sanz were interested in researching the effects of processing instruction across three different production tasks conducted in both the oral and written mode. The research design of their study is summarized in Figure 4-6.

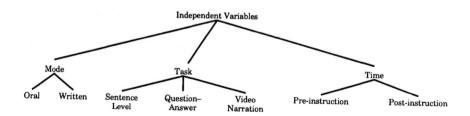

Dependent variables = scores on the three tasks

FIGURE 4-6. Research Design in VanPatten and Sanz (1995).

Results

The researchers conducted a series of *t*-tests on all tasks prior to instruction. These tests revealed no significant differences between the control and the processing groups. After instruction, VanPatten and Sanz conducted a *t*-test on the interpretation task and found a substantial gain in the processing group's performance, similar to the substantial gains made in the previous studies. The control group's pretest/posttest scores were 5.71 and 5.74, respectively, whereas those of the processing group were 5.78 and 11.07. Thus, processing instruction again seemed to alter the strategies used by learners to interpret sentences. We turn our attention now to the results of the production data, examining first the question of mode.

VanPatten and Sanz conducted separate ANOVAs on each task using mode (written vs. oral) and time (pre- vs. posttest) as the independent variables. They also conducted post hoc comparisons based on the results of the ANOVAs. Their findings revealed the following:

1. The processing subjects improved significantly from pre- to posttests on all three tasks whereas the control group did not. The greatest gains showed up in the sentence-level and video-narration tasks.
2. Even though the processing subjects improved, they performed better in the written mode than the oral mode on the sentence-level completion task and the video narration task, but no difference was found for mode on the question-answer task.

In the course of this first set of analyses, VanPatten and Sanz discovered that the question-answer task was yielding problematic data. Even though the processing subjects improved on this task and this improvement was significantly different from pre- to posttesting, the gains were slight. Overall, subjects seemed to be producing few object pronouns in this task, opting instead to repeat full object nouns in their answers. VanPatten and Sanz therefore decided to eliminate the question-answer task from further analyses, concentrating on differences between the sentence-level task and the video-narration task.

Given the results on mode, VanPatten and Sanz conducted another set of ANOVAs in which mode was removed as a variable. They ran two sets of analyses, one on the results in the written mode and another on the results of the oral mode with the independent variables being instruction, time, and task. In this way, they could examine performance across tasks within each mode. The results of the ANOVAs and the subsequent post-hoc comparisons can be summarized as follows:

1. The processing group made significant gains in performance on both the sentence-level and the video narration tasks in the written mode. The control subjects did not.

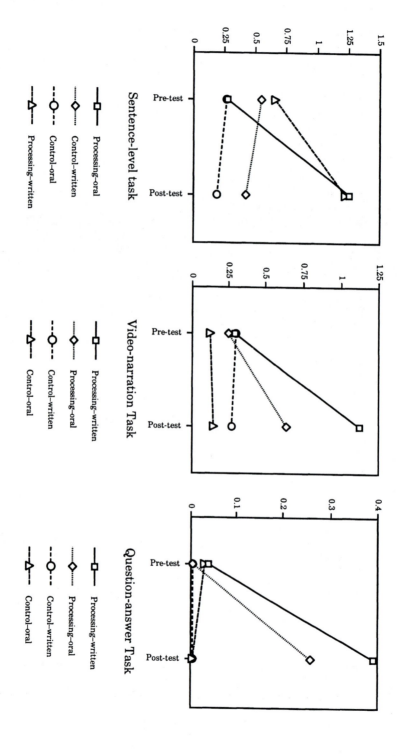

FIGURE 4-7. Results from VanPatten and Sanz (1995) on sentence-level, question-answer, and video-narration tasks showing effects for mode.

108

2. The processing group made significant gains in performance on the sentence-level task but not on the video narration task in the oral mode. The
control group made no significant gains on either task in the oral mode.

The preceding results are presented graphically in Figures 4-7 and 4-8. The
numerical results of the statistical procedures are provided in Tables 4-3
and 4-4.

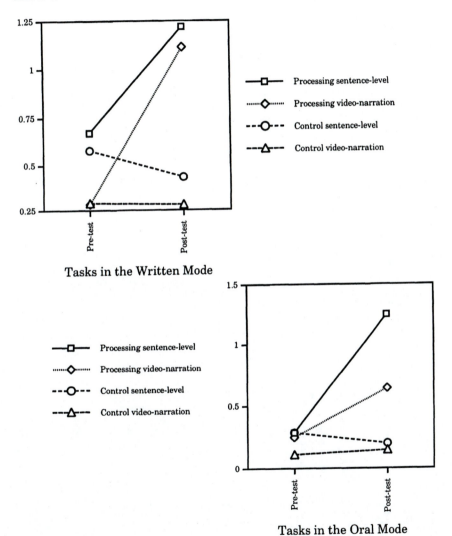

FIGURE 4-8. Results of VanPatten and Sanz (1995) for both sentence-level and video-narration tasks with mode removed as a variable.

Table 4-3. Results of the Analyses of Variance from VanPatten and Sanz (1994) for all Output Tasks in Both Oral and Written Modes

	df	SS	MS	F-value
Sentence completion				
Source of variation				
Instruction	1	9.79	9.79	5.03*
Time	1	4.56	4.56	7.25**
Mode	1	1.93	1.93	6.44**
Time × instruction	1	7.39	7.39	11.50**
Mode × instruction	1	.07	.07	.22
Time × mode	1	.54	.54	1.36
Instruction × time × mode	1	.32	.32	.82
Question-answer				
Source of variation				
Instruction	1	1.14	1.14	4.36*
Time	1	.88	.88	3.98*
Mode	1	.05	.05	1.34
Time × instruction	1	1.08	1.08	4.90*
Mode × instruction	1	.11	.11	2.81
Time × mode	1	.04	.04	1.83
Instruction × time × mode	1	.01	.01	.44
Video narration				
Source of variation				
Instruction	1	5.61	5.61	4.83*
Time	1	3.86	3.89	11.64**
Mode	1	1.71	1.71	4.10*
Time × instruction	1	3.85	3.85	11.60**
Mode × instruction	1	.12	.12	.30
Time × mode	1	.37	.37	1.68
Instruction × time × mode	1	.61	.61	2.76

*$p < .05$; **$p < .01$.

Table 4-4. Results of the Analyses of Variance from VanPatten and Sanz (1994)
for the Written and Oral Versions of the Sentence Completion and
Video Narration Tasks

	df	SS	MS	F-value
Written version				
Source of variation				
Instruction	1	7.82	7.82	4.69*
Time	1	3.95	3.95	6.12*
Task	1	2.17	2.17	4.81*
Time × instruction	1	5.99	5.99	9.27**
Task × instruction	1	.01	.01	.01
Time × task	1	.34	.34	1.36
Instruction × time × task	1	.09	.09	.35
Oral versions				
Source of variation				
Instruction	1	7.29	7.29	5.03*
Time	1	4.46	4.46	9.78**
Task	1	1.94	1.94	7.67**
Time × instruction	1	4.99	4.99	10.95**
Task × instruction	1	.47	.47	1.85
Time × task	1	.57	.57	2.58
Instruction × time × task	1	1.11	1.11	5.02

$*p < .05; **p < .01.$

Discussion of the Findings

The results from VanPatten and Sanz suggest that the effects of processing instruction are observable in the less controlled and more communicative output of learners. Subjects receiving processing instruction made gains on all tasks in the written mode and on two of the three tasks in the oral mode. Only on the oral video narration task did the analyses fail to yield a significant difference between pre- and posttest performance. Nonetheless, as Figure 4-8 shows, processing subjects showed signs of some improvement on this task supporting the conclusion that processing instruction can have an effect on communicative performance.

To be sure, the results reveal that written communicative performance is easier than oral performance and that sentence-level tasks are easier than story telling tasks. But these findings are not a function of instruction since the processing group consistently outperformed the control group. Instead, these findings can be attributed to the different task demands. In the story telling-video narration tasks, for example, not only did subjects have to access their developing systems for word order and object pronouns, they also had to put together entire sentences using correct vocabulary, tense, and so on. Recall that in the sentence-level tasks, subjects only had to produce a short phrase and that vocabulary was provided to them.

So far, then, we have seen evidence that processing instruction is effective with both syntax (object pronouns and word order) and verb morphology. We have also seen that its effects are observable in more communicative and discourse-oriented types of tasks. We will examine one more study in which we see the effects of processing instruction on a different kind of linguistic item.

RESEARCH ON LEXICAL-ASPECTUAL ITEMS: *SER* AND *ESTAR* IN SPANISH

Overview

Cheng (1995) conducted research on the effects of processing instruction and traditional instruction on the acquistion of *ser* and *estar*, the two major copular verbs in Spanish. In her study, processing instruction is related to P1(b) and P1(c) in that the copular verbs are items of low communicative value for second language learners and are redundant features of Spanish. She posed the following research questions as she began her study.

1. Do processing instruction and traditional instruction have the same effects on the acquisition of *ser* and *estar* as measured by the following tasks?
   a. interpretation
   b. sentence completion
   c. composition
2. If there are effects, do these hold over time?

Motivation for the Study

The copular verbs *ser* and *estar* comprise a complex system in Spanish. In many contexts, they are mutually exclusive. For example, only *ser* can be used to connect nouns with noun predicates as in *María es profesora,* "Mary is a professor" and only *estar* is used in progressive constructions, e.g., *María está corrigiendo composiciones,* "Mary is correcting papers." In the case of many adjectives, *ser* and *estar* are both permissable but their selection is determined by the aspectual meaning intended by the speaker. Durative aspect is represented by *ser*, e.g., *Juan es pobre,* "John is poor" meaning John belongs to the class of poor people. Punctual aspect is represented by *estar*, e.g., *Juan está pobre* "John is poor," meaning that John has recently become poor. In English, we might say he is broke or currently without funds. However, with many adjectives, only *ser* or *estar* can be used but not both. For example, adjectives of nationality appear only with *ser,* e.g., *Soy argentino,* "I'm Argentinian." Many adjectives of condition only appear with *estar,* e.g., *Estoy bien,* "I'm fine." In these and other cases, the underlying aspectual meaning of the adjective (e.g., nationality tends to be viewed as durative, whereas condition tends to be viewed as punctual) dictates the use of *ser* or *estar.* In a certain sense, then, *ser* and *estar* are redundant markers of aspect.

In VanPatten (1985b, 1987a), five stages were documented for the acquisition of these verbs with stages III–V quite protracted (see also Fienneman, 1990; Guntermann 1992 for supporting research).

I. Omission of copular verbs (learners simply string together nouns and predicates, e.g., *Juan alto,* "John tall."
II. Acquisition and overextension of *ser.*
III. Acquisition of *estar* with progressive.
IV. Acquisition of *estar* with locatives.
V. Acquisition of *estar* with adjectives of condition and state.

VanPatten hypothesized that *ser* and *estar* are low in communicative value for the learner. In and of themselves, they have no inherent semantic meaning. The choice of *ser* or *estar* is determined by the intended meaning of the adjective or sentence and very often sentences containing these verbs are interpretable via the content lexical items and the context in which the sentence occurs. For this reason, VanPatten argued, learners omit the copular verbs in the early stages; this is reflective of the fact that they may not be attending to them at all in the input. The subsequent acquisition and overgeneralization of *ser* may be owing to frequency in the input; *ser* is three times more frequent than *estar.*

Cheng reasoned that even though *ser* and *estar* are devoid of semantic information themselves, processing instruction might be able to help learners link the use of each copular verb with particular meanings of adjectives and sentences.

The Study

Subjects and Groups

Drawing on the same student population as VanPatten and Cadierno (but once again, not using the same subjects), Cheng randomly assigned six classes of second-year college-level Spanish to one of three groups: control, traditional, and processing. Screening of subjects for background and the use of a 60% cutoff score on the pretests yielded the final numbers of subjects: control ($n = 33$), traditional ($n = 36$), processing ($n = 36$). As in the other studies, subjects were unaware of the comparative nature of the study and were not scheduled to receive any kind of instruction on the copular verbs during the experimental period.

Instructional Treatment

Cheng created two instructional packets for the traditional and processing groups for a two-day instructional period with no homework. The traditional packet was based on the leading second-year textbook *Pasajes,* whereas Cheng developed the processing materials herself. The processing materials reminded students before beginning the activities to "pay attention to the presence of *ser* and *estar,*" because these verbs might help provide clues as to sentence meaning. Focusing exclusively on the use of *ser* and *estar* with adjectives and past participles, her referentially oriented activities included, among other kinds, picture matching activities. For example, students heard either *Pablo es débil* or *Pablo está débil* and had to select from one of two pictures, one in which Pablo is portrayed as a 90-pound weakling and another in which Pablo is sick in bed and weak. Since *ser* seems to be the default verb, Cheng made sure that *estar* was as frequent if not more frequent in the affectively oriented activities. These activities included those in which subjects checked boxes such as "often, sometimes, never" to indicate the frequency with which they find themselves in certain states and conditions, e.g., *Estoy deprimido,* "I'm depressed." Following Lee and VanPatten (1995, Chapter 5) she created a variety of structured input activities for the two-day instructional period.

As in previous studies, she carefully balanced the two packets for number of tokens, vocabulary, activity types, and so on, and checked the items of each packet against her testing materials to avoid a teaching-testing bias. The regular instructors were removed from the classrooms and replaced by a third-party neutral instruction who was not the researcher.

Assessment Tasks and Scoring

Cheng developed various versions of three different assessment tests for use in a split-block design. The first was an interpretation task that contained both aural and written stimulus sentences. There were 10 target items in this test, 4 with *ser* and 6 with *estar*. Cheng used a 1 (correct) versus 0 (incorrect) scoring procedure for this task for a total possible score of 10.

Cheng's second test was a written sentence-level production task in which students had to complete a sentence using *ser* or *estar.* Of the 10 target items, 4 reguired *ser* and 6 required *estar.* Again, she used a 1 versus 0 scoring procedure based on correct use of copula and ignored any other errors in the sentence. The total possible score on this task was 10.

The third test was a guided composition task. Cheng provided subjects with a series of four drawings that narrated a story. Beside each drawing were key words that subjects were instructed to use while writing their "stories." Key words included targeted adjectives as well as other helpful vocabulary to talk about the people, objects, and events in the drawings. Subjects had to use total of 12 adjectives in writing their compositions, five requiring *ser* and seven requiring *estar*.

Cheng used all three tests as both a pretest and two posttests, administered immediately after instruction as well as three weeks later. Using a split-block design with various versions of the tests, Cheng avoided an effect for test item familiarity and test order.

To summarize, Cheng used a research design similar to that of VanPatten and Cadierno. She compared three groups (control, traditional, and processing) in a pretest/posttest format (with only two posttests), but included three rather than two types of tasks: interpretation, sentence-level production, and guided composition. This design is summarized in Figure 4-9.

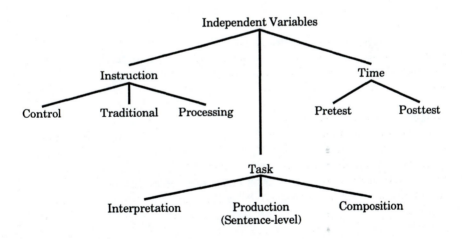

Dependent variables = scores on tasks

FIGURE 4-9. Research design in Cheng (1995).

Results

An ANOVA conducted on the pretest scores revealed no differences between the groups. Separate ANOVAs and post-hoc comparisons on each of the three sets of pre- and posttest scores revealed the following.

1. On the interpretation task, both the processing and traditional groups made significant gains but there were significant differences in the gains made; the processing group gained even more, at least in the first post-test. On the second posttest, the processing group's score dropped to about the same level as the traditional group's but was still significantly greater than their pretest scores.
2. On the sentence production task, both processing and traditional instruction improved significantly and retained this performance across the two posttests.
3. For the composition task, the results were identical to those of the sentence production task: Both processing and traditional improved significantly from pre- to posttests; their performance stayed about the same across the two posttests.

These results are displayed graphically in Figure 4-10 and the statistical results summarized in Table 4-5. Even though the results do not appear to be as dramatic as those in the previous studies, Cheng's analyses of the data revealed consistent significant differences as described in the preceding numbers 1–3.

Cheng pondered the results on the interpretation task since they were not identical to those of previous studies. Although the processing instruction group made significant gains on the interpretation task, so did the traditional group, although its gains were not as great as those of the processing group. Cheng decided to reanalyze the data. She reasoned that *estar* seemed to be the problematic verb in terms of acquisition. Recall that *ser* is acquired early and overextended and that the real problem that confronts learners is the acquisition of *estar.* If this is the case, perhaps perfomance on the *ser* items of Cheng's tasks was masking any effects for *estar.* Cheng thus conducted subsequent ANOVAs and post hoc comparisons on the *estar* items only and obtained the following results.

1. On the interpretation task, only processing instruction made significant gains on both posttests. There was no difference in performance between the traditional and the control groups.
2. On the sentence production task, the results were the same as for the combined *ser* and *estar* data; both processing and traditional instruc-

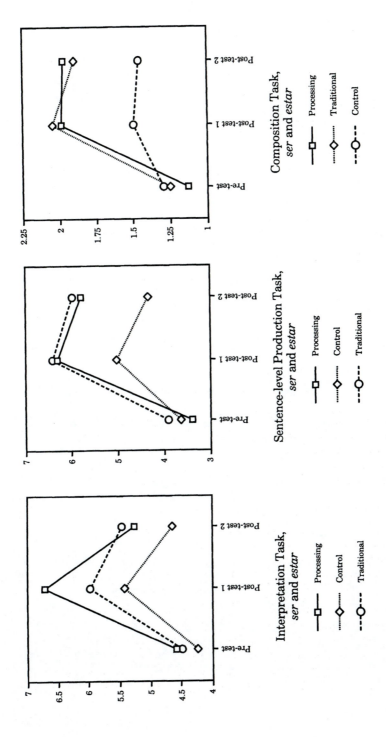

FIGURE 4-10. Results from Cheng (1995) on interpretation, sentence-level production, and composition tasks with *ser* and *estar* combined.

tion improved significantly and retained this performance across the two posttests.

3. For the composition task, all groups scores improved significantly from pre- to posttests, however, the gains made by the processing and traditional group were substantially greater than those made by the control group. There was no difference between the traditional and processing groups.

It seems, then that by analyzing only the *estar* data, Cheng's analyses yielded results similar to those obtained in the previous studies. The results of the reanalyzed data with *estar* only are presented in Figure 4-11. Table 4-6 contains a summary of the statistical results.

Table 4-5. Results of the Analyses of Variance from Cheng (1995) for Combined *ser* and *estar* Data

	df	SS	MS	F-value
Interpretation task				
Source of variation				
Instruction	2	30.64	15.32	8.10**
Time	2	136.28	68.14	37.93**
Time × instruction	4	13.61	3.40	1.89
Sentence production task				
Source of variation				
Instruction	2	63.41	31.71	5.88**
Time	2	260.05	130.02	47.03**
Time × instruction	4	30.32	7.58	2.74*
Composition task				
Source of variation				
Instruction	2	6.15	3.07	6.11**
Time	3	16.93	8.47	26.86**
Time × instruction	4	3.41	.85	2.70*

*$p < .05$; **$p < .01$

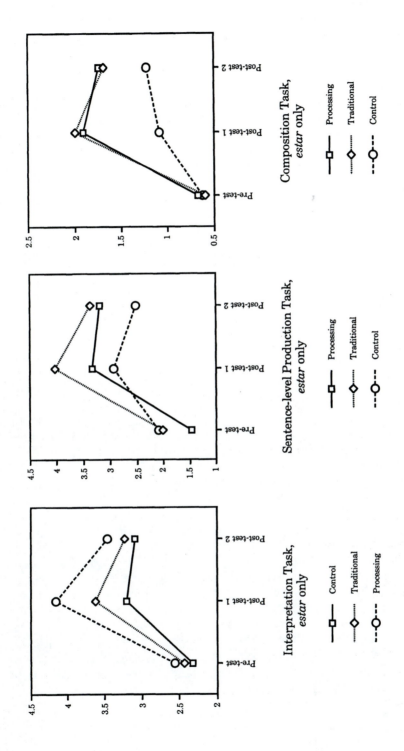

FIGURE 4-11. Results from Cheng (1995) for interpretation, sentence-level production, and composition tasks with *estar* only.

Table 4-6. Results of the Analyses of Variance from Cheng (1995) for *estar* Only Data

	df	SS	MS	F-value
Interpretation task				
Source of variation				
Instruction	2	14.84	7.42	4.04*
Time	2	87.20	43.60	37.81**
Time × instruction	4	5.48	1.37	1.19
Sentence production task				
Source of variation				
Instruction	2	20.28	10.14	2.17
Time	2	121.96	60.98	31.04**
Time × instruction	4	19.46	4.87	2.48*
Composition task				
Source of variation				
Instruction	2	12.19	6.10	3.88*
Time	3	58.72	29.36	51.54**
Time × instruction	4	7.18	1.79	3.15*

*$p < .05$; **$p < .01$

Discussion of the Findings

Cheng's results provide further evidence for the benefits of processing instruction. Using the data on *estar* only, we see that processing instruction results in increased gains on an interpretation task, whereas traditional instruction does not. We see that both processing and traditional instruction result in increased gains on both a sentence-level written production task and a guided composition task. Once again, the effects of processing instruction are observable on output tasks but the effects of traditional instruction are not observable on interpretation tasks.

In spite of the consistent findings regarding processing versus traditional or no instruction, there remains one question that poses potential problems for the previous research. Processing instruction, like traditional instruction, consists of explanation plus some kind of practice, albeit input as opposed to output manipulation. One could conclude that, given the kinds of tasks used in the previous studies, we cannot determine whether or not processing instruction is resulting in a change in the developing system or whether subjects are simply monitoring on the posttests. That is, could the superior performance of the processing groups be due to conscious knowledge gained during the explanation part of the instructional treatment and not to any effect that the activities have in helping to restructure the developing system? We turn our attention to one final study that sets out to research this question.

RESEARCH ON MONITORING: EXPLANATION VERSUS STRUCTURED INPUT VERSUS BOTH

Overview

VanPatten and Oikkenon (1996), conducted a study to find out whether explanation or structured input activities were the causative variables for the previously reported research findings. Using the same materials and assessment tasks as used in VanPatten and Cadierno (1993), VanPatten and Oikkenon divided subjects into three treatment groups. The first received processing instruction exactly as in VanPatten and Cadierno's study. The second received explanation only with no subsequent activities. The third received structured input activities only with no explanation. Their research question was basically the following.

1. In terms of processing instruction, which of the following appears to be the most significant variable in accounting for pretest/posttest gains.
   a. explanation;
   b. structured input activities; or
   c. explanation and structured input activities combined?

Motivation for the Study

All explicit instruction contains explicit information about how the second language works. Be it jargon-ladened or not, this explicit information tells learners about how the language works and, very often, about what *not* to do in order to avoid errors. Processing instruction is not different in this regard. Recall from Chapter 3 that processing instruction consists of explicit information plus structured input activities and that the explicit information is of two types: (1) how the language works; (2) what natural processing strategies may be getting in the way of acquiring a particular form or structure. As Krashen (1982) has argued, this explicit information can be stored only as concious knowledge in the form of a Monitor, a device that edits output when task demands allow for monitoring to happen. For the Monitor to be engaged, Krashen has claimed, the single most important feature of task demands is time (Krashen, 1982, p. 89). He states that it takes real processing time to remember and apply conscious knowledge or rules when making output. For this reason, it is difficult for learners to engage the Monitor during ongoing conversation and timed written tasks, whereas it is easy (but not guaranteed) for learners to engage the Monitor with simple written tasks (e.g., filling in a blank) and untimed writing activities.

According to Krashen's view, then, we must look at the interpretation and sentence-level production tests used in processing research as possible tasks in which learners might easily Monitor. Is the explicit and therefore conscious knowledge possessed by the learners after receiving explanation responsible for the gains observed in the research reported in previous sections of this chapter? Since the tasks do not resemble spontaneous conversation in any way, many are written sentence-level tasks, it would seem reasonable the ask to what extent our results are due to Monitoring. What this would mean in terms of research is that if Monitoring were responsible for the outcomes of previous research, then providing learners with explicit information only should reveal similar patterns of gains from pre- to post-tests as in VanPatten and Cadierno (1993). However, if the use of explicit information in and of itself is not responsible for observed gains, then two possibilities exist. The first is that the structured input activities themselves are responsible. As bonafide comprehensible input, if structured input alone is responsible for the results, then we have further support that acquisition is indeed happening—or beginning to happen—under processing instruction. The other possibility is that the explicit information and the structured input activities together are responsible for the gains, in which case we would have to argue for a weak interface position similar to that taken by Ellis (1994). He argues that conscious knowledge is used in a secondary manner by learners to "notice" new forms and structures. The conscious knowledge enables learners to engage bottom-up processing that he claims is necessary for acquisition. (We, too, believe that bottom-up processing is necessary; that is what is meant by attention to meaning and form during input processing. However, as we stated in Chapter 2, consciousness need not be linked to this bottom-up processing.)

To summarize, if conscious knowledge and Monitoring are responsible for the observed gains after processing instruction, then we should see these gains in two groups: a group that receives explanation only and one that receives regular processing instruction (explanation plus structured input activities). We should see no gains in a group that receives structured input only. If, however, conscious knowledge and Monitoring are not responsible for the observed gains, then we should see no gains in an explanation-only group but instead should see gains in a group receiving only structured input as well as one receiving regular processing instruction.

THE STUDY

Subjects and Groups

Subjects from a local Champaign secondary school participated in the study. All were in their second year of Spanish courses in a somewhat traditional program in which mastery of grammar is emphasized and only minor importance is placed on skill development. As in VanPatten and Cadierno (1993), a background questionnaire and pretests were administered to arrive at the final data pool. All subjects had to be native speakers of English with no outside contact with Spanish. All had to score less than 70% on the pre-tests to be included in the subject pool. The final total of subjects was 59, divided into the following groups: Explicit Instruction Only ($n = 22$); Structured Input Activities Only ($n = 20$); Processing Instruction ($n = 17$).

Instructional Treatment

Processing Instruction consisted of the materials used in VanPatten and Cadierno (1993) as well as VanPatten and Sanz (1995). No alterations were made in the content of the materials and no homework was allowed (all packets were picked up at the end of each class day). Instruction was spread over three days—as opposed to only two—given the shorter class periods that generally mark secondary schools in the United States.

Explanation Only consisted of the explanatory sections of the materials used in VanPatten and Cadierno with no activities. No homework was allowed and again packets were picked up at the end of each day. Subjects read the explanation as the instructor reviewed it and provided examples. Subjects were encouraged to ask for clarification or repetition if necessary. As in the Processing Instruction treatment, the Explanation Only group received their explanation over the course of three days, each day's explanation and information corresponding to the explanation given in the Processing group on that day. Since no activities were used, the rest of class time was taken up with games and activities unrelated to object pronouns and word order.

Structured Input Only consisted of the activities contained in the materials used in VanPatten and Cadierno with no explanation preceding them. The instructor merely began the activities and said whether or not students had made appropriate selections or not (during the referential activities). In a picture identification activity, for example, the instructor would read a sentence and students would select picture *a* or *b* to match to what they had understood. If students identified the correct picture, the instructor said "Good. Let's continue with the next one." If students selected the incorrect picture, the instructor would merely say "No. The picture that goes with what you just heard is _____." At no time did the instructor inform students about rules or object pronouns in Spanish and if students asked explicitly about what they were to learn the instructor said, "Let's just see if at the end of the week if you've gotten it." Moreover, the instructor did not call students' attention to the object pronouns or word order and did not single them out in any way. As for the other two groups, the treatment lasted for three days and the activities conducted each day corresponded to those that were used in Processing Instruction on each day. No homework was given and all packets were picked up at the end of each day.

The instructor was the same for all three groups. She was an inexperienced teacher-in-training who had not worked with processing instruction or structured input previously.

Assessment Tasks and Scoring

The assessment tasks consisted of the same interpretation and sentence-level production tasks as used in VanPatten and Cadierno (1993), but only one posttest was used. This posttest was administered the day after the instructional treatments were completed. Two versions of each task were used in a split-block design (some learners got version A as the pre-test and B as the post-test and some got version B as the pre-test and A as the post-test. The scoring procedure was the same as that in VanPatten and Cadierno's study.

Results

An ANOVA conducted on the subjects pretest results revealed no significant differences between the groups on either task. Once again, any observed effects are attributed to treatment.

The ANOVA conducted on the interpretation task revealed a significant main effect for instruction (Explicit vs. Structured Input Activities vs. Processing), time (pre- vs. posttest) and a significant interaction between instruction and time. A comparison of means revealed that the observed effects were caused by both processing and structured input only making significant gains from pre- to posttests on the interpretation task. The explicit only group made no gains.

On the production task, the ANOVA yielded a significant main effect for instruction (Explicit vs. Structured Input Activities vs. Processing) and time (pre- vs. posttest) but no interaction. All groups gained from pre- to posttest. However, the gains made by the structured input only group and the processing group were greater than those made by the explicit only group. The preceding results are summarized in Figure 4-12 and Table 4-7.

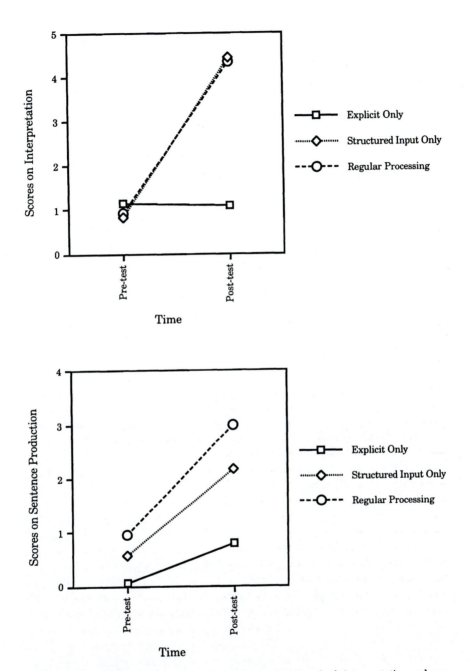

FIGURE 4-12. Results of VanPatten and Oikkenon (1996) on both interpretation and sentence-level production tasks.

Table 4-7. ANOVA Summaries for Both Interpretation and Production Tasks in
VanPatten and Oikkenon (1996)

	df	SS	MS	F-value
Interpretation task				
Source of variation				
Instruction	2	63.896	31.948	9.056**
Time	1	159.947	159.947	50.322**
Time × instruction	2	88.785	44.392	13.967**
Production task				
Source of variation				
Instruction	2	48.556	24.278	3.220*
Time	1	62.348	62.348	12.881**
Time × instruction	2	9.066	4.533	0.937

*$p < .05$; **$p < .01$

Discussion of the Findings

The results from VanPatten and Oikkenon suggest that Monitoring is not the causative or signficant variable for the results observed in processing instruction. First, the explicit only group did not make significant gains from pre- to posttests on the interpretation task. Just as important to note, however, is that the structured input only group performed as well as the regular processing group and made significant gains from pre- to posttests. Although all groups improved on the production task, the gains made by the structured input only and the processing group were greater than those of the explicit only group. These findings suggest that it is the actual structured input itself and the form-meaning connections being made during input processing that are responsible for the observed effects in the present as well as previous studies.

We must temper this conclusion, however, by noting that in the structured input only group, learners were provided with negative feedback during referential activities (i.e., "No. The correct picture is *b*. Let's try the next one.") It is possible that learners formed conscious knowledge on their own as a result of these types of activities that interacted with subsequent referential as well as affectively oriented activities. If this is the case, then we could conclude that explicit knowledge does aid input processing and that is why the structured only and the regular processing groups performed in similar fashion across the experiment. What we can rule out, it seems, is the role of the Monitor on its own. That is, it is unlikely that Monitoring is a significant factor in the research reported on in this chapter. If it were, the explicit only group should have made more observable gains in the VanPatten and Oikkenon study.

CONCLUSION

In the five studies that we have reviewed in this chapter, the effects of processing instruction are consistently observable. Not only do learners receiving processing instruction gain in the ability to process input better, but also their developing system is affected such that they can access the targeted linguistic features when making output. This is the case with a variety of linguistic items, and in the VanPatten and Sanz study we saw that the effects of processing instruction extend to a variety of output tasks. In addition, the findings of VanPatten and Oikkenon suggest that it is the engagement in structured input activities within processing instruction that is the most significant variable; explicit information (explanation) does not appear to be critical.

On the other hand, traditional instruction appears to have effects only on output tasks. Subjects who received traditional instruction consistently gained in their ability to produce the targeted linguistic features, but they did not gain in their ability to interpret the targeted linguistic item. This is a curious finding that we will explore along with other issues in the next chapter.

In spite of the fairly robust picture that is emerging on the effects of processing instruction, one major question has not been addressed: Are the effects of processing instruction long-lasting? In two studies, VanPatten and Cadierno (1993) and Cadierno (1995), studied the effects for processing instruction held over a one-month period. However, the researchers did not conduct any testing at a later time. In Cheng (1995), the effects for processing instruction held over a period of three weeks, with no further testing conducted. Other research, for example, White (1991) showed that the effects of traditional instruction may wear off within one year, whereas in other studies instruction has proved to be more durable, for example, White et al. (1991) It would seem, then, that future research on processing instruction should address this important issue.

chapter **5**

CHALLENGES AND IMPLICATIONS

INTRODUCTION

Both input processing and processing instruction raise a number of issues for acquisition and instruction unaddressed in previous chapters. These issues include possible challenges to processing instruction as well as implications of input processing and processing instruction for theory building in second language acquisition research. The present chapter presents a discussion of these issues.

The first issue concerns input processing and problems in the acquisition of syntax as described by researchers using Universal Grammar (UG) as a framework. UG has gained increasing visibility in both first language and second language research since the mid-1980s (see, e.g., Eubank, 1991; Towell & Hawkins, 1994; White, 1989). Perhaps of all the linguistically oriented theories that contain an innatist component, UG has become the most widely discussed and debated (see Eubank & Gregg, 1995; and the responses by Schumann, Jacobs, & Pulvermüller). Even in general reviews of second language acquisition intended as textbooks (Ellis, 1994; Gass & Selinker, 1994) discussions of UG have come to be standard. Because of its relative prominence in the discourse on second language acquisition, we have opted to review the relationship of UG (to the exclusion of other frameworks) to input processing in this chapter. Since theories often compete for explanatory power, it is not unreasonable to ask what input processing has to offer second language acquisition theory that UG cannot account for. The argument will be that both input processing and UG are *complementary* components of a larger more general model of second language acquisition and use.

The second issue is the role of first language transfer. Because input processing does not incorporate (as of yet) a role for first language transfer but transfer is a recognized phenomenon in second language acquisition, it would seem that input processing offers an incomplete account of second language acquisition. As in the case of UG, we will show that both input processing and first language transfer form part of a larger more general model of second language acquisition.

The third issue involves the teachability of "meaningless" linguistic features. Since input processing is largely concerned with form-meaning mappings, how can processing instruction work effectively on those elements of language which are devoid of meaning? The argument will be that processing instruction can affect the acquisition of these features and that this is empirically testable.

The chapter will conclude with an examination of the differential outcomes of traditional and processing instructional treatments reported in Chapter 4. The issue here is why processing subjects improve in both interpretation and production but the traditional subjects do not. The resolution of this last issue will come from the general model of language acquisition that forms the basis of the present book.

UNIVERSAL GRAMMAR, SYNTAX, AND INPUT PROCESSING

Research within the framework of UG and current government-binding theory as applied to second language acquisition is concerned with abstract properties of syntax. Although both P3, the first noun strategy, and the research of VanPatten and Cadierno (1993) concern syntax since they deal with the processing of word order by second language learners, the syntax of the first noun strategy is not the same kind of syntax as that which concerns specialists in UG and government-binding theory. Those working within UG are (principally) concerned with such matters as (1) how abstract principles constrain the acquisition of grammar; and (2) parameter setting versus (3) parameter resetting (i.e., first language transfer of parameters and the subsequent resetting of the parameter to the second language value). Most research on UG and second language acquisition has concentrated on the latter two issues and the first question that arises is what input processing has to do with UG and parameter resetting. A follow-up question is the extent to which a model of input processing instruction can account for observed phenomena in second language acquisition that UG cannot. Each of these questions is taken in turn. Since the role of UG is taken up in considerable detail in a number of other publications (e.g., Eubank, 1991; Towell & Hawkins, 1994; White, 1989) the discussion here will be brief for illustrative purposes only.

Universal Grammar and Language Acquisition

In order to understand the potential relationship between input processing and UG, understanding how UG is conceptualized is necessary. What is necessary also is to examine some of the issues addressed by UG-related research in second language acquisition.

As currently formulated, UG is an innate knowledge source. It consists of a set of abstract principles about language in addition to information on the possible syntactic variations (parameters) that languages can follow. Because this knowledge is innate and universal in all human beings, UG constrains first language acquisition by allowing children to entertain only certain possibilities about the syntax of languages. These constraints are called principles. A classic example of a universal principle is X-bar Theory, which says that an X^0 (also called a "head") must project onto an X' (the head plus its complement) and that the X' must in turn project onto an XP (the X' plus its specifier). As an example, a N (noun) such as *dog* must project onto an N' (the noun plus its complement) as in *dog on a leash*. This in turn must project onto an NP (the N' plus a specifier) such as *the dog on a leash*. (Note: "must project" is a bit misleading. As we all know, a noun phrase can be as simple as *the dog* (*See the dog?*) In UG theory, the projections within syntax are there, they just might not have words that fill them.) Since word order in languages is not a mere serial ordering of elements in that words group together to make phrases, this principle provides for a hierarchical internal structure of sentences. Thus children "know" that the language they are learning has phrase structure and all they need to do is acquire lexical items and categorize them as nouns, verbs, prepositions and so on so that they can project them into the correct phrase structure (see, e.g., the discussion in Radford, 1990).

Likewise, parameters within UG "inform" children about the possibilities for a given syntactic principle. Linguists have discussed a number of parameters: the head parameter, the null-subject parameter, and the verb raising parameter, to name a few. These parameters permit certain options and, since the parameters are part of UG, children possess the knowledge that the language they are learning will have one of the options set forth by the parameter. In the case of verb raising, for example, children "know" that the language will either allow verbs to raise or not. In certain analyses (Pollock, 1989), a clause (sentence) contains an abstract representation such as that in Figure 5-1. Lexical verbs such as *eat, drink, hit,* and so on—as opposed to auxiliaries and modals such as *have, do,* and *can*— are generated under the V' node, specifically under V^0. Agreement features for person and number are located under Agr^0 whereas tense features are located under T^0. According to Pollock, languages either allow lexical verbs to raise and land in Agr^0 to get agreement features while picking up tense features along the way (as the arrows indicate in Figure 5-1), or they do not. French is one language that does. Movement of the verb root *boi-* into T⁰ and Agr⁰ is indicated by the arrows. English, on the other hand, does not allow lexical verbs to raise; hence the asterisk in front of the verb root *drink-*. This one syntactic parameter accounts for a number of phenomena that differ between the two languages: placement of negators (e.g., *John drinks not coffee with milk./Jean ne boit pas de café au lait.*), placement of frequency and manner adverbs (*John drinks often coffee with milk./Jean boit souvent du cafee au lait.*), requirement of *do*-support in English (John does not drink coffee with milk./*Jean ne fait pas boire du café au lait.*), among others. According to the theory of parameters within UG then, children's internal processors should notice from the input data whether their language allows verb raising or not and they will set the parameter accordingly. For example, children learning Spanish get consistent data about verb movement with simple yes–no questions that contain subject-verb inversions, e.g., *Volvió tu*

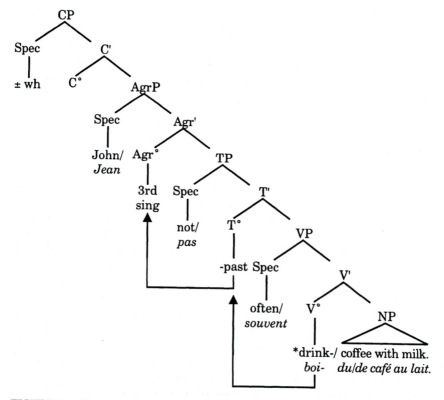

FIGURE 5-1. The structure of clauses showing differences between English and French with verb-raising.

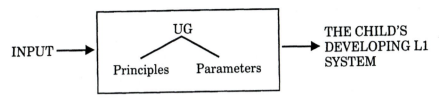

FIGURE 5-2. The role of UG in first language acquisition.

hermano de la escuela? Did your brother get back from school? (Literally: Returned your brother from the school?) According to generative approaches to syntax, this inversion is due to the verb moving and taking a spot higher than the subject in the syntactic tree. On the other hand, children learning English never get data in which lexical verbs occupy a spot before subjects, e.g., *Did your brother get home?/*Did get home your brother?/*Got home your brother?*

UG, then, is a knowledge source that restricts the range of possibilities for syntactic configuration in a language. Principles dictate particular aspects of syntax, whereas parameters allow for a narrow range of options for a given syntactic rule. These principles and parameters lie in wait for the relevant linguistic data that will trigger their instantiation. In Figure 5-2 we summarize in simple form the manner in which UG works in first language acquisition (based on White, 1989).

The exact role of UG in adult second language acquisition is a matter of debate. Three possibilities exist. The first, that UG is no longer active in second language acquisition and that learners use more general (but still abstract) cognitive problem-solving strategies to develop a functioning second language system. The second possibility is the opposite; that second language learners have access to UG just like children acquiring their first language. The third possibility is that second language learners have access to UG but that the parameters instantiated for the first language they possess can interfere with this access. If we assume for the moment that second language learners have access to UG in some way (with or without first language mediation), then just like first language learners they must possess "internally derived hypotheses" (Towell & Hawkins, 1994, p. 247) that interact with the input data. Thus, learners entertain particular hypotheses about the second language that are subsequently supported or rejected by the input data. An English-speaker learning French as a second language, for example, might come to the task of acquisition not expecting verbs to raise. The value of the parameter at the initial stage would be [-raising]. That learner will (re)set the verb-raising parameter to [+raising] once the evidence from subject-verb inversion, adverb placement, placement of negation, and so on, is encountered.

What the preceding accounts of both first and second language acquisition have in common is that UG interacts with *input* data. In Figure 5-2, for example, there are no intervening processes that mediate between UG and input. As White stated,

> The function of the input data in language acquisition is to help to fix one of the possible settings. This is called triggering. In other words, the input helps to make the choice between various settings (White, 1989, p. 29).

Thus, the instantiation of principles and parameters is dependent upon input. There is a problem in this conceptualization. It assumes that data in the input are readily available for UG's use. It further assumes that the internal structure of every utterance is processed and is readily available to UG. The problem is that these assumptions cannot be supported. According to the model of input processing developed in Chapter 2, learners' processing of input results in a reduced and sometimes altered subset of the input data. These data, called intake data, are subject to further processing (accommodation) that, when it occurs, can lead to restructuring of the developing system. In this view, the developing system uses intake data and not input data for growth. If UG forms part of the internal mechanisms used in *restructuring* of the grammar, it follows that UG must make use of intake data; that is, *UG does not operate on input data for the construction of the developing system; instead, it operates on intake data.*

In order to make our case, we must first recall the general model of second language acquisition and use outlined earlier in this book. In this model, second language acquisition and use consists of distinct sets of processes as shown in Figure 5-3. The first set of processes filters the input data in particular ways resulting in intake data. These data are then accommodated or not by the developing system with subsequent restructuring of the system depending on the nature of the intake data. If we combine Figure 2-3 from Chapter 2 with Figure 5-3, we can expand the general model. The result is Figure 5-4. At this point the only role for UG is in the identification and assignment of head lexical categories since every learner must be able to assign a word a category such as noun and verb during initial processing. If not, acquisition simply couldn't happen.

$$\text{input} \xrightarrow{\text{I}} \text{intake} \xrightarrow{\text{II}} \text{developing system}$$

I = input processing
II = accommodation, restructuring

FIGURE 5-3. Sets of processes in second language acquisition.

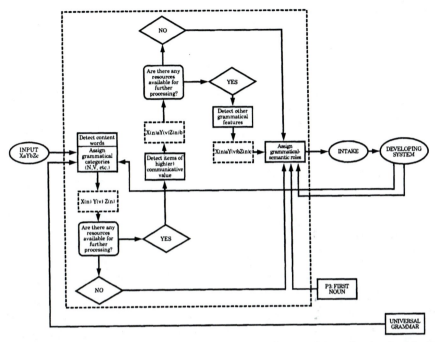

FIGURE 5-4. An expanded model of second language acquisition and use showing the role of input processing.

(In Figure 5-4, and subsequent figures, *XYZ* represent content lexical items, whereas *a, b,* and *c* represent functors, morphology, and other surface grammatical features.)

It is now possible to examine a rather straightforward case on the interaction of UG with intake. Recall that the model of input processing developed in Chapter 2 entails a push for meaning and that based on the limited capacity for processing input data learners will process lexical items in the input before anything else. The model also predicts that learners will process grammatical markers in accordance with the role they play in contributing to sentence meaning during comprehension. In Figure 5-4, if the processing resources are depleted in the first go round, that is, the processing of lexical items uses up all available resources, then all that is delivered as intake for further processing are content lexical items with some kind of serial ordering. This means that the developing system would not receive sufficient, if any, data about most prepositions, auxiliary verbs, copular verbs, verb inflections, agreement markers, and so on. If UG is interacting almost exclusively with lexical items in the beginning, then the prediction would be that the lexical categories of syntax would develop before the functional ones. As Zobl (in press) points out, this is precisely what happens. He states:

> Lexical categories in thematic positions are in evidence long before functional categories appear in functional positions. In earlier stages of L2 acquisition, the latter are either absent, treated like lexical categories or are unanalyzed parts of chunk-learned items. Moreover, the acquisition of the lexical-thematic component of L2 grammars seems virtually assured while the same cannot be said of the functional component (p. 24).

If UG interacted directly with input, then we would expect the functional elements of syntax to appear much earlier than they do. Because they do not, our conclusion is that the relevant data for UG are the reduced intake data and not the full input data.

There are more complicated scenarios that also suggest an interaction of UG with intake and not input. In Towell and Hawkins (1994, pp. 132–138) the authors reviewed UG and competing cognitive accounts of second language acquisition to demonstrate the superiority of UG in accounting for certain developmental stages. Towell and Hawkins reviewed the following cases: (1) acquisition of obligatory subjects in English by speakers of null-subject languages; (2) acquisition of preposition stranding by learners of English; (3) acquisition of object pronouns in French by speakers of English. In each case, although UG accounts for some very important acquisitional phenomena, there are other phenomena left unexplained.

In the case of the acquisition of obligatory subjects, Towell and Hawkins cited research in which obligatory subject pronouns are acquired in the following order:

referential ⟶ quasi-argument ⟶ expletive.

This means that referential pronouns such as *they* and *she* are acquired before quasi-argument pronouns such as *it*, as in *it is raining,* which in turn are acquired before the expetive pronoun *it* of *it is impossible to tell.* Although one could argue that different pronoun types form part of UG (i.e., this knowledge is built into UG), Towell and Hawkins pointed out that UG cannot account for the order in which the pronouns are acquired. Although frequency in the input may be a factor, as noted by Towell and Hawkins, we could also claim that the pronouns are processed differentially in the input. Subject pronouns, such as *they, she,* and others, are lexical items of high communicative value since they encode referential meaning and since verbs in English do not encode for person-number. Learners must use them in processing input to account for subject shifts in utterances they hear or even to establish a referent at the onset of connected discourse. For example, compare the following sets of utterances with and without referential pronouns and it becomes clear how learners would rely on them early on to establish reference.

> *Without referential pronouns:* Called Pedro yesterday. Talked for at least an hour. Said were coming to dinner.
> *With referential pronouns:* I called Pedro yesterday. We talked for at least an hour. He said you were coming to dinner.

Quasi-arguments and expletives are devoid of communicative value since they do not encode any referential meaning. As argued earlier, the principles in Chapter 2 would predict that referential pronouns would be detected and made available as intake before the other pronouns. This is supported by the fact that *it* as a referential pronoun in the example *it is on the table* is acquired before the other types of pronouns. When *it* functions as a referential pronoun, it has clear communicative value and the form-meaning mappings produced by input processing are clear and unambiguous. In terms of the ordering of quasi-argument and expletive pronouns, frequency may indeed be a factor here because there is no theoretical reason why these two pronouns should not be acquired at the same time. (Towell and Hawkins do not provide information on the relative lag time of the acquisition of these pronouns so that quasi-arguments and expletives could be acquired close together.)

For preposition stranding, Towell and Hawkins cited Bardovi-Harlig's (1987) study. She found that learners first acquire structures without WH-movement such as *She talked to whom?* This is followed by a stage in which learners front a WH-element but no preposition is present, for example, *Who did she talk?* Towell and Hawkins could account for this by suggesting that there is a problem with licensing, that learners have not learned that P^0 (a preposition) can govern an empty category in English. Accordingly, learners delete the preposition to avoid violating the theory of licensing and empty categories. By deleting the preposition, the verb may govern the empty category left behind by the moved WH-element. Although this fits within the theory of UG, Towell and Hawkins noted that it is problematic in that the process of deletion is not entirely understood. They then go on to suggest that perhaps learners have not correctly subcategorized verbs, such as *talk,* as an indirectional transitive verb requiring a prepositional phrase. The question is, why wouldn't learners have subcategorized this verb correctly? The answer may lie in that the prepositions do not form part of the intake data in the early stages at all and thus deletion is a misconceptualization of the facts. The relatively low communicative value of the preposition *to* may result in that the first round of processing of content lexical items in the input ignores it. Thus, learners may be providing intake data to UG that resembles *I talk Jerry* and *We talk him the phone last night.* Note that *talk* can also appear in the input without prepositional phrases: *She talks a lot*; *He talks too fast.* In short, the developing system may be getting data in which *to* is absent. In this way, we have an explanation for why learners might have problems in initially determining the subcategorization of verbs like *to*. The question arises, then, as to why learners' first stage includes the preposition, for example, *She talked to whom?* There are two possibilities here. The first is that the phrase *to whom* does not consist of two separate words but is actually one unit *towhom*. In spoken English, *to whom* would form a natural breath group and if any natural junctures are inserted into an utterance, speakers would separate *to whom* from *talk* and not *whom* from *talk to*. In this way, *towhom* is initially encoded as an NP and not a PP during input processing. UG is thus given a consistent picture that the verb *talk* does not require a prepositional phrase. The only way we can confirm that *towhom* forms a unit for the early stage learner is to show that *whom* is never used by learners without *to* in unmonitored speech during this stage of development. In any event, the developmental stages can be explained if we assume that UG is operating on intake data and not input data.

A second explanation lies in that the first stage of production is largely monitored and is not an accurate reflection of underlying competence. That is, when learners produce *She talked to whom?* in the early stages, this very well could represent an example of monitored output. This receives some support if one considers that the naturally occuring input to learners is not likely to contain very many samples of *to whom*. More likely is that learners would hear utterances such as *She talked to who?* Their use of *to whom*, then, in the early stages could reflect something that they were taught and are attempting to use, but that natural stages of acquisition assert themselves with increasing exposure to input.

A third case in which UG cannot explain all of the observed phenomena in acquisition involves object pronouns in French. Towell and Hawkins reported that the first stage of object pronoun production in French by speakers of English involves placement of the pronoun after the verb: *J'ai reconnu le,* "I recognized him." This is followed by a stage akin to Bardovi-Harlig's data on preposition stranding in which the pronoun is missing: *J'ai reconnu.* In the third stage learners incorrectly place the pronoun between the auxiliary verb and the past participle: *J'ai le reconnu.* Towell and Hawkins could explain the overall developmental stages by arguing for the availability of null-objects in UG. That is, UG allows for null-objects and that perhaps learners of French have determined that V^0 (a verb) can license *pro* (an empty category in which a pronoun would appear in a language like English). Assuming the validity of this argument, Towell and Hawkins point out that a UG account begs at least one question: "Why aren't learners able to recognise the preverbal location of object pronouns as soon as they notice they are absent postverbally?" (p. 138). This question can be handled if it is assumed that the object pronouns are not processed in the input and therefore do not make their way into intake. Two points are relevant here. First, in French subject pronouns are obligatory and are always preverbal in declarative sentences. Thus, assigning the subject role to the first noun results in correct grammatical and semantic role assignment so that the problem learners of Spanish encounter does not enter here (see the discussion in Chapter 2). Second, full object nouns are invariably post-verbal as in *J'ai reconnu Marie,* "I recognized Mary," as are object pronouns with affirmative commands: *Faites-le,* "Do it" *Lis-le,* "Read it." Initial intake data might very well be giving UG information that French is strictly VO (Verb-Object) regardless of whether O is a full noun or a pronoun. Now, recall that as learners progress in acquisition, their developing system takes on a greater role in sentence processing. This is depicted in Figure 5-4 by the arrow leading to and from the developing system to various aspects of input processing. If the developing system has determined that French is SVO, then this knowledge may constrain the processing of sentences after the earliest of stages. Note that the input data contain very weak and nonsalient object pronouns in preverbal position: The vowel is generally schwaed and the object pronoun elides with verbs that begin with a vowel: *Je le vois de temps en temps,* "I see him from time to time;" *Je l'ai vu hier soir,* "I saw him last night." In spoken French, the vowel of the object pronoun may be weakened to the point that it is imperceptible. At the same time, French allows consonant clusters in initial position that are unheard of in English with the result in the cases of cliticized object pronouns being sequences such as *lv* for *lvois.* If the learner cannot perceive the preverbal object pronoun in the earlier stages then the input string *Je le vois* may become intake resembling *Je vois* since the developing system would push an SV assignment based on its interpretation that French is SVO. This intake datum is accompanied by the meaning "I saw him" in which case the mechanisms involved in the instantiation of principles and parameters of UG have no choice but to consider that null-objects are permissible in French. Here, then, our account involves the initial word order data that are delivered to UG as intake coupled with problems in acoustic perception of object pronouns in spoken French. That learners perceive and produce object pronouns initially in post-verbal position is accounted for by input utterances containing commands with post-verbal object pronouns. (A second explanation of the first stage in which object pronouns are produced post-verbally was also used to discuss the acquisition of preposition stranding. That is, the initial output of learners could be heavily monitored, resulting in the use of French lexical items mapped onto English syntax. Learners may be putting together surface features of language that they have consciously learned, but since they are not generating the sentence based on an acquired competence, the syntax of the sentence ends up resembling the syntax of an English sentence. More succinctly, learners could be "thinking in English" in the earlier stages and adding on French lexical items during output processing.)

In each of the preceding three cases of acquisition (subject pronouns in English, preposition stranding in English, object pronouns in French), UG can account for various developmental phenomena successfully but certain parts of the acquisitional picture are not accounted for. Assuming that UG operates on intake data rather than input data, then a more fully developed account of the observed phenomena emerges. To be sure, acoustic saliency and the phonetic realization of the input speech stream became important in describing the results of input processing in the second and third cases of acquisition. Once again, a complete model of input processing must incorporate principles that involve acoustic features of input (see the brief discussion in Chapter 2) that is left to future research for the time being.

Although Towell and Hawkins did not explicitly claim that UG operates on intake data, they hint at this in their model of second language acquisition. In their model, input data must pass through short-term memory before it can be compared to the internally derived hypotheses—hypotheses that originate in either UG or the first language. They state that short-term memory "is the mechanism which determines the information available to long-term memories" (p. 250). Later, they state that input data may not serve to confirm or deny the internally derived hypotheses, citing that the developing system may be insufficient to aid in the processing of an utterance or "because short-term memory is *limited in capacity* [and] learners are often unable to decipher the internal structure of utterances when these are first heard in context" (p. 253, emphasis added). What Towell and Hawkins suggested, then, is congruent with the present proposal; that input processing may deprive UG of the information it needs for the accurate construction of the syntactic component of the second language.

Returning to Figure 5-4, we are able to situate UG into our general model of second language acquisition and use. The result is Figure 5-5. In this model, UG's primary role lies in the second set of processes, accommodation, and restructuring. After input processing creates intake data, the intake is processed subsequently by those mechanisms that compare the data to the principles and parametric values in UG. Depending on the state of the developing system, the data may confirm some aspect of syntax, force the restructuring of the system, or may be irrelevant to a current hypothesis about the syntax. In short, whether or not a hypothesis generated by UG is confirmed or rejected depends on the intake data UG receives and not the input that the learner hears.

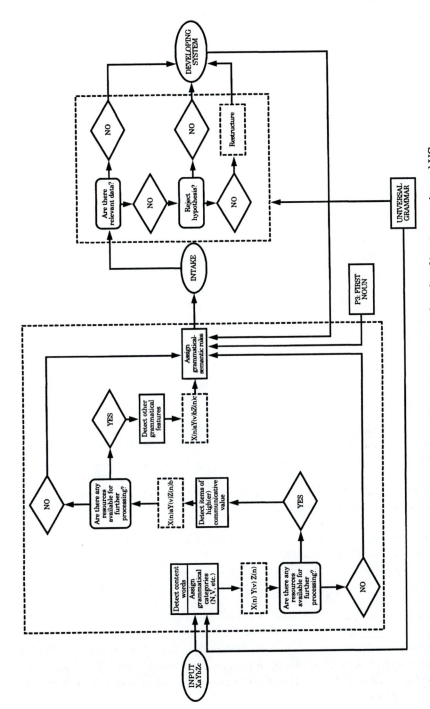

FIGURE 5-5. An expanded model of second language acquisition and use showing the roles of input processing and UG.

First Language Transfer

In the previous section, we focused on the relationship between UG and input processing in the creation of the syntactic component of the learner's developing system. However, first language transfer is a widely recognized phenomenon in second language acquisition (e.g., Gass & Selinker, 1983, 1992; Odlin, 1989; White, 1989). What is its relationship to input processing? Given that the first language is a knowledge source in the same way that UG is, it seems logical that its role also would lie in determining the initial hypotheses that a learner would entertain about the syntax of the second language. For example, suppose that a speaker of English with a strict SVO word order undertakes the acquisition of Spanish. The first language may generate an initial hypothesis that Spanish also is strictly SVO. Input processing, relying on the first noun strategy and unable to attend to grammatical markers related to case in the input, would deliver intake to the developing system in which subjects always seem to be preverbal and objects postverbal. The result would be that the initial hypothesis is confirmed and indeed the interlanguage of English speakers of Spanish is heavily if not exclusively SVO, even when pronouns are used (see Andersen, 1983; VanPatten, 1987b, for discussion).

As another example, suppose that a speaker of Spanish learning English begins with the hypothesis that negation is preverbal; more specifically, that a simple negator is placed in front of a finite verb as it is in Spanish (e.g., *No hablo español,* "I don't speak Spanish"). If this is the case, then the structure of the IP (Inflectional Phrase) is hypothesized to be something different than it is in English or that rules of movement in which verbs and negators must travel together holds as it does in English. As soon as the learner processes input containing the following sentences, the hypothesis is confirmed—or, at least, not rejected. (Note: As will be discussed later, the learner is probably not attending to the support verb *do* in early stages of acquisition, hence *do* is placed in brackets.)

1. No talking!
2. [Do] not write on the paper.
3. [Do] you study or not (study) at night?

Thus, the processed data appear to conform to the hypothesized structure of negation which in turn is based on the first language.

As one final example, let's return to verb raising. Recall that lexical (not auxiliary) verb raising is a parametric value in UG such that some languages allow it (are [+raising]) and some do not (are [-raising]). Spanish is [+raising], whereas English is [-raising]. Also recall that important relevant data for the internal processors concerned with UG includes subject-verb inversion.

Languages that are [+raising] allow some kind of subject verb inversion at least in yes/no questions. Thus Spanish allows *¿Comieron los chicos ya?* Did the boys already eat? (Literally: Ate the boys already?) with the verb preceding the subject and indeed occupying sentence initial position. What is also of importance here is that Spanish does not have true modals or auxiliaries like English. Thus, there are no lexical equivalencies of *can, could, will, would, might, do,* and so on, since the work of these modals is taken up in verb inflections. Spanish does have an equivalent of have, *haber,* which functions similarly to its English counterpart: Have you eaten? *Has comido?* Spanish also has a verb *poder* that translates into English as *can* but is not an auxiliary; in fact, the semantic field of *poder* is much wider than English's *can.*

Now, what happens when Spanish speakers begin acquiring English? If they begin with the internal hypothesis that English is [+raising] just like Spanish, what kind of data do they get? If learners incorrectly subcategorize *can* in English as a lexical verb rather than as an auxiliary auxiliary, then some of the initial data they get would lead them to conclude that English (may be) [+raising]. *Can you come?, Could you pass the salt?* are sample data with subject-verb inversion.

Amending Figure 5-5, the first language as a hypothesis generating knowledge source for the developing system is depicted in Figure 5-6. The first language is not seen to act directly during input processing. Instead, it interacts with intake data to shape the developing system.

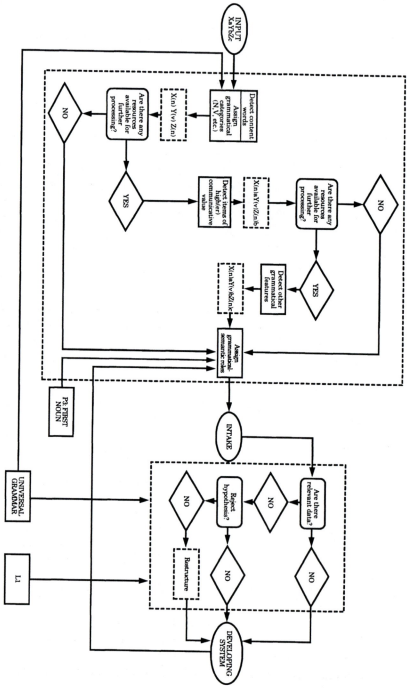

FIGURE 5-6. An expanded model of second language acquisition and use showing the roles of both UG and L1.

144

Summary

It should be clear from the preceding discussion that input processing and UG are not placed in an either/or opposition as is often the case with UG and a competing theory. What Figure 5-5 suggests is that both input processing and UG play a role in the nature of the developing systems of second language learners. By incorporating a role for input processing in delivering intake to UG, we can account for various phenomena in acquisition that at first glance seem to fall outside the scope of UG theory. In addition, the first language is also accounted for in that it is a knowledge source that generates hypotheses. As in the case of hypotheses generated by UG, the first language-generated hypotheses interact with the intake data for confirmation or rejection (see Figure 5-6).

COGNITIVE ACCOUNTS VERSUS FORMAL LINGUISTICS

The previous discussion lays the groundwork for a number of other issues related to the role of input processing in developing a theory of second language acquisition. It is true that the model of input processing developed in Chapter 2 is essentially cognitive. Utilizing constructs from cognitive psychology such as limited capacity, attention, detection, and so on, a model emerged that predicts the processing of linguistic features based on their role in providing cues to sentence meaning for second language comprehenders. In addition, the cognitive processing of sentences involving the first noun strategy, lexical semantics, and grammatical cues in the input forms the basis for the developmental nature of grammatical-semantic role assignment in second language input processing.

Second language researchers working within the framework of generative linguistics have been critical of cognitive accounts of second language acquisition. These criticisms claim that UG can account for the same phenomena that cognitive accounts attempt to explain. In addition, these criticisms show that UG can account for more phenomena. Following the argument of "parsimony in explanation," critics argue that UG is preferred because it accounts for a wider range of phenomena. Finally, these criticisms argue that cognitive approaches often propose ad hoc or poorly motivated principles that are untraceable to any theory. (Another criticism, not as important to the present discussion as the preceding but certainly important in the field of second language research, is that cognitive approaches very often do not have a theory about the thing being acquired. That is, as theories about learning, cognitive approaches do not first attempt to adequately describe that which is being learned: language.)

Towell and Hawkins (1994, Chapter 4) claim that common to all cognitive approaches is that learners initially decode, analyze, store, and produce language using general cognitive strategies similar to those proposed by Slobin (1973) and other first language researchers. To make their case that these accounts are inadequate, Towell and Hawkins examine two approaches in detail. The first is Pienemann's model (see, e.g., Pienemann, 1987) and the second is Wolfe Quintero's (Wolfe Quintero, 1992). The first model is an attempt to account for the developmental stages of the acquisition of German word order. In it, Pienemann made use of *conservatism* in developing the Canonical Order Strategy. Accordingly, learners attempt to conserve the dominant word order of the simple input strings they have been exposed to, for example, SVOAdv in the case of German. To account for the next stage, Pienemann used *perceptual saliency* in developing the Initialization and Finalization Strategy. At this stage, learners can move sentence initial and final elements since they are more perceptually salient, for example, adverbs can be fronted now so that both SVOAdv and AdvSVO are possible. However, in German, finite verbs appear in second position in simple declarative sentences such that once adverbs can be fronted, learners should be producing AdvVSO or AdvAuxSOV constructions that they do not. To account for this delay in acquisition, especially of the Aux and V separation, Pienemann made use of the concept of *continuity*.

Wolfe Quintero (1992) attempted to account for the developmental stages of WH-question formation. In her account, Wolfe Quintero similarly made use of conservatism to account for the initial invariant stage as well as continuity to account for nonseparation of prepositions from WH-elements. To account for subsequent stages of development, Wolfe Quintero posited an interaction among various cognitive mechanisms: *uniqueness* to account for one-to-one mappings, *cumulative development* to account for the building of one stage on another, *generalization* to account for the lack of exceptions, and *pre-emption* to account for confirmation or denial of a hypothesis.

In their evaluation of the preceding models, Towell and Hawkins noted that the cognitive principles do not account for certain observed facts, most important, first language influence. For example, continuity would not predict that French speakers of English would consistently separate verbs and objects by intervening adverbs from the earliest stages of development. That is, continuity would predict only "John drinks coffee often" in the earliest stages and not the attested "John drinks often coffee." In a similar vein, the Canonical Order Strategy would not predict the outcome of Hulk's (1991) study in which first language speakers of Dutch learning French as a second language initially utilize Germanic word order and not an SVO order. In both examples, the general cognitive principles would not predict first language transfer and instead would predict that all learners regardless of first language would exhibit identical and invariant first stages of acquisition.

Thus there exists a situation in which cognitive models are pitted against

UG and that the weaknesses of the cognitive models become salient as one begins to explore their predictions and compare these to the observed facts in a variety of acquisitional situations. Assuming that these cognitive approaches are indeed inadequate (and by no means would everyone agree), what is to prevent the model of input processing in the present book from succumbing to the same criticisms? There are three reasons why the present model of input processing is not vulnerable to the criticisms leveled at other cognitive models. First and foremost, *input processing is not an account of learning; it is an account of what kind of intake data are made available for learning.* Recall that in, Figure 5-3, acquisition and use are separated into three distinct sets of processes. Input processing is only concerned with those processed depicted by I in the figure and is not intended to account for any other processes. In their criticism of Pienemann's and Wolfe Quintero's cognitive models, Towell and Hawkins claimed that these models are intended to account for the *decoding, analysis, storage,* and *production* of language. In other words, these models attempt to account for the sets of processes in Figure 5-3 in addition to how learners create output. Because input processing is concerned with a much more reduced set of phenomena, the present model does not make predictions about how the developing system creates a syntactic component nor about what the output of learners may look like.

The second reason that our model of input processing is not subject to the same criticism as more general cognitive accounts of second language acquisition is related to the first reason; unlike cognitive models that are all encompassing, input processing is not in competition with a theory based on UG. As Figure 5-5 illustrates, input processing and UG concern distinct aspects of second language acquisition. The first section of this chapter contains a discussion of how the cognitive aspects of input processing interface with the grammatical knowledge contained in UG. By claiming that UG operates on intake data, the present model incorporates a mutually compatible if not conspiratorial relationship between input processing and UG.

The third reason that our model of input processing is not vulnerable to the criticisms of Towell and Hawkins is that first language transfer is allowed to play a role in the creation of the developing system. As seen earlier, both UG and the first language can play a role in generating the initial hypotheses that a learner entertains about the second language. This role of the first language is clearly depicted in Figure 5-6.

To summarize, the principles of input processing outlined in Chapter 2 do not attempt to account for all aspects of acquisition; they do not comprise a total model. Instead, they form part of a model that attempts to account solely for the derivation of intake data. Accommodation, restructuring, output generation, and other aspects of language acquisition and use must be accounted for by other theories or models. In this way, input processing does not overgenerate predictions. When placed with UG and first language transfer in a larger more general model, a more complete account of acquisition emerges.

PROCESSING INSTRUCTION AND SYNTAX

The previous discussion on the relationship between input processing and the development of syntax leads us to several questions about processing instruction.

1. Because processing instruction's aim is to push learners to attend to elements in the input that they might otherwise miss, and since input processing is principally concerned with creating form-meaning relationships, how can processing instruction be used to teach items that are meaningless?
2. A related question concerns lexical versus functional categories. Zobl claims that the nature of functional categories renders them unteachable. Thus explicit instruction cannot aid in their development. Is this true for processing instruction as well?

Processing Instruction and Meaningless Items: An Example from Verb Raising

The first question is most easily observed in the problem of verb raising in second language acquisition. White (1992) and Trahey and White (1993) showed that first language speakers of French have difficulty in eliminating the error of placing manner and frequency adverbs between verbs and objects when learning English. Because they assume that verbs can raise in English, these learners continue to make errors of the type noted in a previous section of this chapter: *John drinks often coffee. *Mary watches quietly television. However, they do learn the permissible locations of adverbs in English that are disallowed in French. Thus, they can produce *John often drinks/has often drunk coffee*. Even with explicit instruction and negative feedback, errors of the type *John drinks often coffee* are persistent. And input flooding (i.e., providing the learners with input over a short period of time that is saturated with correct positive evidence in the input) does not seem to help either (Trahey & White, 1993). Assuming that this error is due to the differences between French and English regarding the verb raising parameter, we can see why traditional instruction and negative feedback would not remedy these learners' error. As Schwartz (1993) points out, UG can interact only with data processed in the input; it is not a knowledge source that can interact with explicit conscious knowledge about language. Likewise, the input flooding would not work if the input did not contain the right triggers. Note that adverb placement is a result of the verb raising parameter and may not be a trigger for it. Thus one could question why adverb placement would be the correct instructional target if indeed the issue is that learners must restructure their grammars and reset the parameter to [-raising].

The question is whether processing instruction can provide better intake for UG so that the correct verb parameter can be reset. Note that verb raising and adverb placement cannot be considered meaningful aspects of language. Both *John often drinks coffee* and *John drinks coffee often* (as well as the erroneous *John drinks often coffee*) all refer to the same referential set of circumstances. The different placement of the adverb, then, does not contribute to sentence meaning during comprehension and it is not clear how the form-meaning mappings created by input processing are relevant here. Before examining this last issue, it is necessary to review some facts about verb raising first.

Recall that the clause has an abstract structure like that in Figure 5-1. Lexical verbs originate under V^0 and move up to pick up tense and then land in Agr^0 to pick up agreement in French. This accounts for placement of adverbs (sentence 1 following) and negators in French to the right of finite verbs (sentence 2) as well as subject verb inversion that includes a further raising of the verb into C^0 (sentence 3). (The use of Jean as a topic marker in sentence 3 is irrelevant here; note that the verb and subject pronoun are inverted.)

1. $[_{IP}$ Jean$[_{AGR}$boit$_i$ $[_{VP}$ souvent $[_{V'}e_i$ du café au lait.$]]]]$
2. $[_{IP}$ Jean$[_{AGR}$boit$_i$ $[_{TP}$ pas $[_{VP}$ souvent $[_{V'}e_i$ du café au lait.$]]]]]$
3. Jean $[C'$ boit$_i$ $[_{IP}$ il $[_{VP}$ souvent $[_{V'}e_i$ du café au lait.$]]]]$

In English, the features in Agr^0 and T^0 lower into the VP so that lexical verbs do not move up. The negator *not* blocks the lowering of Agr^0 features so that *do* is forced. This accounts for the placement of adverbs and negation to the left of verbs in English (sentences 4 and 5, respectively). *Do* can move into C^0, which accounts for yes/no questions (sentence 6).

4. $[_{IP}$ John$[_{AGR}$ e_i $[_{VP}$ often $[_{VP}$ drinks coffee with milk.$]]]]$
5. $[_{IP}$ John$[_{AGR}$ does $[_{TP}$ not $[_{VP}$ often $[_{VP}$ drink coffee with milk.$]]]]$
6. $[_{CP}$ Does$_i$ $[_{IP}$ John$[_{AGR}$ e_i $[_{VP}$ often $[_{VP}$ drink coffee with milk.$]]]]$

If the initial hypothesis of learners of French is that English raises all verbs, then the real clue to UG that English does not allow verb raising is not the location of adverbs or negators but the presence of *do*. This analysis receives support from Lightfoot (1993) who demonstrates that the evolution from [+raising] to [-raising] as Old English become Modern English is accompanied by the appearance and use of *do* as a dummy verb. In discussing the period of change from 1475 to 1550, Lightfoot says

> Each insertion of a periphrastic *do* to carry inflectional markers represents a case where the V-to-I [verb raising] operation has not applied, so a steady increase in the distribution of *do* entails fewer and fewer instances of V-to-I; the two operations are mutually incompatible (p. 207).

In terms of second language acquisition, if learners are attending to all the lexical elements in an input string then, the sequence *do* + NEG + VERB should tell the learner that Agr is structured differently in English and therefore verbs cannot raise. In short, *do* is the trigger to reset the parameter to -raising. The question then becomes whether or not learners are detecting *do* in the input.

Research on the acquisition of negation in English suggests that learners do not attend to *do* as a separate lexical item in the input in the early and intermediate stages (for overviews of research on negation, see Ellis, 1994; Larsen-Freeman & Long, 1991; among others). Stage 1 of negation consists of NEG + phrase, for example, *No go, No come tonight*. Stage 2 consists of the beginnings of clause structure with NEG being sentence internal and placed before the verb, for example, *I no come tonight*. At this same time and also in Stage 3, we see the use of *don't* as an unanalyzed chunk that replaces *no* as the principle negator, for example, *I don't come tonight; He don't study*. At the same time, we see that in the acquisition of questions in English, *do* is absent in the first two stages. These data suggest that the intake data delivered to UG does not contain a separate *do* that would force an analysis of English Agr⁰ and T⁰ that is more target-like. The absence of *do* in the intake is predicted by our model of input processing. As an item of essentially little or no communicative value (the root *do* carries no semantic information), it is easily skipped during input processing and its contraction with *not*—an item of high communicative value because it is the only item in the utterance that will indicate to a learner that something is being negated—in the forms of *don't* and *doesn't* easily could lead the mechanisms of input processing to deliver to UG the following information: *no, not, don't,* and *doesn't* are allomorphic variations of NEG.

If this analysis is correct and *do* is the key to forcing a rejection of verb raising by French speakers learning English, then the instructional question is whether or not processing instruction can aid in attention paid to *do* in the input. It would seem that this is possible. Since *do* carries both Agr features and T features, both of which are meaning-based, then these might be exploited in the form of processing instruction to get learners to actively attend to and detect *do* during structured input activities. As an example, structured input activities could encourage learners to attend to *do* versus *does* to get person and/or *do/does* versus *did* to get tense (see the instruction in Cadierno, 1995, in Chapters 3 and 4). It would then be up to UG to analyze *do* correctly after it is initially detected and the form-meaning mappings are made. The outcome of this scenario is, of course, an empirical question and one which depends on the proposed differences between Agr⁰ and T⁰ in French and English.

Processing Instruction and Functional Categories

The question of lexical versus functional categories is related to the first question of teaching meaningless features of language. Zobl (m.s.) claims that functional categories are "semantically shallow or vacuous" observing the lack of semantic meaning and purely grammatical nature of linguistic items such as complementizers, conjunctions, and the auxiliary *do*. Citing research from adult first language sentence and lexical processing, Zobl also claims that the processing of functional categories is "automatic and encapsulated" and thus is separate from the processing of lexical categories. Based on this analysis, he argues that the acquisition of functional categories is not responsive to any kind of explicit knowledge derived from explicit instruction and that this is counter-theoretical to the weak interface positions (e.g., Ellis, 1993; Sharwood Smith, 1991).

At first glance, Zobl's claim appears to be correct. However, there are a number of problems with the argumentation. First, it is not clear that adult first language sentence processing research is directly relevant to second language acquisition. Presumably, automatic processing is preceded by repeated and consistent controlled processing (McLaughlin, 1987). From this one could argue that the automatic processing of functional elements in adult first language research might not have started out as automatic processing in child first language acquisition. It would seem logical, then, that second language learners have to build up the automatic processing of functional elements as well. Second, it is also not clear that functional elements and their functional projections in syntax are consistently semantically vacuous. In the case of prepositions, the well-known end of Lincoln's Gettysburg Address is evidence against this: "A government OF the people, FOR the people, and BY the people shall not perish...." Complementizers can be signals of tense, agreement and/or mood features. In Spanish, for example, the complementizer *que* obligatorily heads tensed clauses with finite verbs. Contrast the following:

(1a) *Quiero leerlo.*
    I want to read it.
(1b) *Quiero que lo leas.*
    I want you to read it.
(2a) *Creo ser inteligente.*
    I believe I'm intelligent.
(2b) *Creo que eres inteligente.*
    I believe you are intelligent.

In cases such as these, *que* can serve as additional cue during input processing that a tensed verb is coming and that there may be a subject (person-number) shift.

In the case of *do*, it is important to recall that this support verb is a tense and agreement carrier. Although the verb itself is semantically empty, in a certain sense there is semantic information encoded into this word. *Does,* for example, signals third-person singular, whereas more important (from the learners point of view) *did* signals past, whereas *do/does* signal nonpast. Thus, the tense contrast between *Did you always pay attention?* and *Do you always pay attention?* rests on processing the verb *did/do* in the input.

The problem with many functional elements as we saw in Chapter 2 is not that they are semantically empty; it's that they often co-occur with other lexical items or markers rendering them redundant, for example, *Did you always pay attention **in high school**?* Thus, the relative lack of communicative value of functional elements is owing to built in language redundancy and not any inherent semantic vacuousness. (For this reason, we distinguish between semantic value and communicative value.) According to the model developed in Chapter 2, they are likely to be consistently attended to and detected at a later stage of development in input processing if at all. Since the examples just cited are no different in communicative value from such things as tense markers and copular verbs, and whereas there is evidence that processing instruction has a beneficial effect on these latter items (Chapter 4), it would seem reasonable to conclude that the acquisition of many functional elements could be speeded up by processing instruction. As in the case of verb raising, the effects of processing instruction on functional elements is an empirical question.

REMAINING ISSUES RELATED TO PROCESSING INSTRUCTION

One of the more interesting findings from VanPatten and Cadierno (1993), Cadierno 1995), and Cheng (1995) is the differential effect that processing instruction and traditional instruction seem to have. In these studies the traditional group's performance improved only on production tests. The processing group's performance, however, improved both on interpretation and production. Why this difference? One obvious factor to examine is task familiarity caused by instructional treatment. The production task was one with which the traditional group was familiar, because there were several activities based on it in this group's instructional treatment. The interpretation task was not familiar to them since it did not form a part of the instructional treatment. A logical conclusion would be that task familiarity is a factor in the outcome. However, the results of the processing group on both tasks leads us to question the role of task familiarity. Recall that the processing group had familiarity with the interpretation task but no familiarity with the production task. In processing instruction, learners are engaged in structured input activities, not output activities. Yet, the processing group was able to perform as well as if not better than the traditional group on a task with which the former had no familiarity but the latter did. Thus, task familiarity can account for one set of results (those of the traditional group) but not the other (those of the processing group).

These differential outcomes can be explained by the general model of second language acquisition and use that informs this book. In Figure 5-3, the developing system is seen to be a result only of input processing and the accommodation of intake and the restructuring of the system. In the expanded version of Figure 5-6, we have seen that input processing, UG and the first language all play roles in the formation and growth of the developing system. Processing instruction is a response to this model. Since its aim is to alter or improve input processing, the result is better intake for the mechanisms that accommodate data and restructure the system. Our claim is that processing instruction is an approach that can directly affect acquisition (in Krashen's sense) since it is input oriented; in short, the data are appropriate for the processes responsible for acquisition of grammar. Traditional instruction, on the other hand, does not provide input data to learners. It consists of explicit knowledge plus various kinds of output practice. Thus, traditional instruction should not affect acquisition.

If we expand the general model of language acquisition to include output processing, then we get something like Figure 5-7. Here we see that the creation of output involves a set of processes that tap the developing system in some way. One conclusion regarding the results of the research on processing versus traditional instruction is that the processing subjects were performing with acquired knowledge, knowledge that has become part of their developing system. For this reason, they were able to improve on both interpretation and production tasks. Since traditional instruction does not affect acquisition, our conclusion is that the traditional subjects performed the production task with learned knowledge, knowledge that did not form part of their developing system. Here is where task familiarity may play some role. Given that the traditional group practiced producing the target items

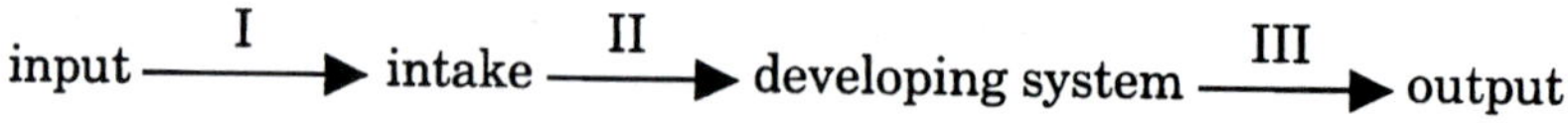

$$\text{input} \xrightarrow{\quad I \quad} \text{intake} \xrightarrow{\quad II \quad} \text{developing system} \xrightarrow{\quad III \quad} \text{output}$$

I = input processing
II = accommodation, restructuring
III = access

FIGURE 5-7. Three sets of processes in second language acquisition and use.

with their explicit knowledge, it is feasible that they gained some ability to use this knowledge on the fairly simple and time-controlled tasks used in the studies. In effect, they were Monitoring to borrow terminology from Krashen. However, whereas they had no practice with interpretation tasks, they could not effectively Monitor on these timed interpretation tasks.

CONCLUSION

This chapter has examined several challenges to input processing and processing instruction: the relationship of input processing to UG and to first language transfer; how our model of input processing differs from other cognitive frameworks that attempt to explain acquisition; whether or not "meaningless" features of language can be taught via processing instruction; and the differential outcomes of traditional and processing instruction on interpretation and production tasks. Unlike other approaches to theory building, the proposed model of input processing is not offered in lieu of UG and first language transfer as accounts of second language acquisition. Instead, it is offered as a companion aspect of a general model of language acquisition and use. In this more general model, input processing is responsible for delivering intake that is then used to confirm or reject hypotheses generated by UG or the first language. In this way, the combined efforts of input processing, UG, and first language transfer account for more phenomena in second language acquisition than any one could alone.

The discussion in this chapter has led to a number of questions about the limits and effects of processing instruction. Can meaningless items be taught via processing instruction? Are the results of processing instruction attributable to Monitoring? Does processing instruction actually affect the acquired system, what is called in the general model the developing system? An examination of these questions reveals that they are empirical questions and imminently researchable. Because processing instruction is predicated upon psycholinguistic mechanisms and a theory of communicative value (that is, the relationship between linguistic form and referntial meaning during the development of second language comprehension), and because it is not opposed to current linguistic theory but can draw on that theory to examine problems in acquisition, processing instruction lends itself to experimental evaluation. In both theory building and in practical application, experimental evaluation is a critical and necessary process in the advancement of the field.

chapter **6**

EPILOGUE

These are both interesting and exciting times for language instruction. In terms of theory, we have come a long way in our understanding of the nature of second language acquisition since the 1960s. We have moved from simple accounts of how learners internalize a grammatical system to an understanding that acquisition is componential, multidimensional, and richly complex. We have a flourishing research field that explores everything from UG in second language acquisition to the nature of reading comprehension to the role of anxiety in (un)successful acquisition. Our more complete understanding of second language acquisition has led a number of us to rethink grammar instruction and to engage in active research on its effects. For the first time we are beginning to make concrete suggestions for grammar instruction that are grounded in both theory and research.

It is the aim of this book to explore the theory, research, and implications of processing instruction. To this end we have examined in some detail the nature of input processing in second language acquisition. We have reviewed an instructional approach that makes use of insights from input processing and we have examined in some detail five investigations on the effects of processing instruction. We concluded with an examination of how input processing fits into the larger picture of second language acquisition and use, and thus, how it works in tandem with other factors such as UG and first language transfer. In so doing we have addressed potential criticisms of both input processing and processing instruction from a formalist perspective.

There is no doubt that input processing and processing instruction will face additional challenges as researchers turn more of their attention to how learners attend to input data to create intake. There is no doubt that adjustments in the model outlined in Chapter 2 and elaborated on in Chapter 5 will occur. Perhaps a different model will replace it. As committed researchers and scholars, we should welcome these challenges, for they represent progress in the fields of both second language acquisition and second language teaching. Indeed, at various points along the way, we have suggested what paths continued research on input processing and processing instruction might follow.

Before concluding, there are two points that the reader should consider. The present book has focused on one particular type of grammar instruction and has attempted to support it with theory and research. The reader should not conclude from this focus that we are advocating an abandonment of the communicative classroom. We are not advocating that processing instruction occupy all of instructors' and learners' time to the exclusion of interaction, reading, and other components of a communicative approach. Instead, as Lightbown and Spada (1993) state, "we need to develop a better understanding of how form-focused instruction can be most effectively incorporated into a communicative framework" (p. 106). To this end, not only do we need to continue research that explores the psycholinguistic underpinnings of processing instruction and its relative effects, but we also need to ask ourselves questions of a much more practical nature: Can and should processing instruction occur outside the classroom, say, as homework? Does it need to be brought into the classroom? Because processing instruction is input-based, can computers deliver effective processing instruction? Pursuing questions such as these will help instructors and curriculum developers maximize communicative language use during the rather minimum amount of time that language students spend in the classroom.

A second point worth bringing to the reader's attention concerns the reaction of instructors to processing instruction. Processing instruction admittedly is a radical alternative to traditional approaches to grammar instruction. Focused on input and devoid of a mechanical stage, how does the experienced instructor perceive processing instruction? I recall having been invited to a large state university to speak to a group of graduate teaching assistants and experienced faculty about my research on processing instruction. After a 45-minute presentation of some of the research presented in Chapter 4 of this book, I entertained questions from the audience. A graduate teaching assistant with some experience raised her hand and asked, "So, you don't believe in explicit instruction or a focus on form then?" After overcoming my initial surprise, I responded that processing instruction *was* a focus on form. As my eyes swept the audience, I realized that she was not the only person who had concluded that processing instruction was "implicit" instruction. At a reception held later I fielded a number of related questions. It seems that a number of people in the audience had filtered my talk through the schema that they associate(d) with Krashen and comprehensible input: no instruction in grammar. To talk of input processing, then, and processing instruction, was seen as to offer yet another version of the Natural Approach.

As researchers, we must take care as to how the nonresearching and possibly uninformed teacher interprets our research. Traditional instruction is very much alive, at least in foreign language teaching in the United States. Teachers dutifully explain, drill, pass out worksheets, administer discrete-point tests of grammar, all in the name of helping learners internalize ("master") the grammar. And if we are absolutely honest, we would admit that most of language teaching in the United States is not communicative at all; it is grammar teaching with some communicative interaction added on. If research on grammar instruction such as that contained in the present book eventually is to have an impact on language teaching, then we must be cognizant of the beliefs and practices of teachers. It would be interesting indeed to be alive in the year 2050 to see what has happened to processing instruction. Assuming it survives the theoretical and research challenges that may come its way, will it survive the challenge of existing teaching practices and beliefs? My hope is that it will.

REFERENCES

Andersen, R. (1983). Transfer to somewhere. In S. M. Gass & L. Selinker (Eds.), *Language transfer in language learning* (pp. 177–201). Rowley, MA: Newbury House.

Bardovi-Harlig, K. (1987). Markedness and salience in second language acquisition. *Language Learning, 37,* 385–407.

Bardovi-Harlig, K. (1992). The use of adverbials and natural order in the development of temporal expression. *International Review of Applied Linguistics, 30,* 299–320.

Bates, E., & MacWhinney, B. (1989). Functionalism and the competition model. In B. MacWhinney & E. Bates (Eds.), *The cross-linguistic study of sentence processing* (pp. 77–117). Cambridge: Cambridge University Press.

Bates, E., MacWhinney, B., Caselli, C., Devescovi, A., Natale, F., & Venza, V. (1984). A cross-linguistic study of the development of sentence interpretation strategies. *Child Development, 55,* 341–354.

Bavin, E. L., & Shopen, T. (1989). Cues to sentence interpretation in Warlpiri. In B. MacWhinney & E. Bates (Eds.), *The cross-linguistic study of sentence processing* (pp. 185–205). Cambridge: Cambridge University Press.

Berne, J. (1989). The effect of increased comprehensibility on learner's ability to consciously attend to content and form. Unpublished manuscript. Manuscript, University of Illinois at Urbana-Champaign.

Bever, T. G. (1970). The cognitive basis for linguistic structures. In J. R. Hayes (Ed.), *Cognition and the development of language* (pp. 279–362). New York: Wiley.

Binkowski, D. D. (1992). *The effects of attentional focus, presentation mode, and language experience on second language learner's sentence processing.* Unpublished doctoral thesis, University of Illinois at Urbana-Champaign.

Blau, E. K. (1990). The effect of syntax, speed and pauses on listening comprehension. *TESOL Quarterly, 24,* 746–753.

Bransdorfer, R. (1989). Processing function words in input: Does meaning make a difference? Paper presented at the annual meeting of the American Association of Teachers of Spanish and Portuguese, San Antonio.

Bransdorfer, R. (1991). Chap. 2: Review of the literature. *Communicative value and linguistic knowledge in second language oral input processing.* Unpublished doctoral thesis, University of Illinois at Urbana-Champaign.

Bybee, J. (1991). Natural morphology: the organization of paradigms and language acquisition. In T. Huebner and C.A. Ferguson (Eds.), *Crosscurrents in Second Language Acquisitions and Linguistic Theories* (pp. 67–91). Amsterdam: John Benjamins.

Cadierno, T. (1992). *Explicit instruction in grammar: a comparison of input based and output based instruction in second language acquisition.* Unpublished doctoral thesis, University of Illinois at Urbana-Champaign.

Cadierno, T. (1995). Formal instruction from a processing perspective: An investigation into the Spanish past tense. *Modern Language Journal, 79,* 179–193.

Cadierno, T., Glass, W. R., Lee, J. F., & VanPatten, B. (1991). Processing tense in second language input: Lexical cues versus grammatical cues. The University of Illinois at Urbana-Champaign.

Carlson, R. A., & Dulany, D. (1985). Conscious attention and abstraction in concept learning. *Journal of Experimental Psychology: Learning, Memory, and Cognition, 11,* 45–58.

Carr, T. H., & Curran, T. (1994). Cognitive factors in learning about structured sequences: Applications to syntax. *Studies in Second Language Acquisition, 16,* 205–230.

Carrell, P. (1985). Facilitating ESL reading by teaching text structure. *TESOL Quarterly, 19,* 727–752.

Ceci, S. J., & Howe, M. J. A. (1983). Metamemory and effects of intending, attending, and intending to attend. In G. Underwood (Ed.), *Aspects of consciousness* (pp. 147–164). New York: Academic Press.

Cheng, A. (1995). *Grammar instruction and input processing: The acquisition of Spanish ser and estar.* Unpublished doctoral thesis, University of Illinois at Urbana-Champaign.

Chomsky, N. (1988). *Language and problems of knowledge: The Managua lectures.* Cambridge, MA: MIT.

Corder, S. Pit. (1967). The significance of learners' errors. Republished in Corder (1981) *Error analysis and interlanguage.* Oxford: Oxford University Press.

Dienes, Z., Broadbent, D., & Berry, D. (1991). Implicit and explicit knowledge bases in artificial grammar learning. *Journal of Experimental Psychology: Learning, Memory, and Cognition, 17,* 875–887.

Dulany, D., Carlson, R., & Dewey, G. (1984). A case of syntactical learning and judgment: how conscious and how abstract? *Journal of Experimental Psychology: General, 113,* 541–555.

Ellis, R. (1990). *Instructed Second Language Acquisition.* Oxford: Basil Blackwell.

Ellis, R. (1993). The structural syllabus and second language acquisition. *TESOL Quarterly, 27,* 91–113.

Ellis, R. (1994). His new book with Oxford.

Ellis, R. (1995). Interpretation tasks for grammar instruction. *TESOL Quarterly, 29,* 87–106.

Ervin-Tripp, S. M. (1974). Is second language learning really like the first? *TESOL Quarterly, 8,* 11–128.

Eubank, L. (1991). *Point/Counterpoint: Universal Grammar in the Second Language.* Amsterdam: Benjamins.

Eubank, L., & Gregg, K. (1995). Et in amygdala ego? UG, (S)LA, and neurobiology. *Studies in Second Language Acquisition, 17,* 35–58.

Faerch, C., & Kasper, G. (1986). The role of comprehension in second language learning. *Applied Linguistics, 7,* 257–274.

Finnemann, M. D. (1990). Markedness and learner strategy: Form- and meaning-oriented learners in the foreign language context. *Modern Language Journal, 74,* 176–187.

Garrett, N. (1991). Theoretical and pedagogical problems of separating "grammar" from "communication." In B. Freed (Ed.), *Foreign Language Acquisition Research and the Classroom* (pp. 74–87). New York: D.C. Heath.

Gass, S. (1989). How do learners resolve linguistic conflicts? In S. Gass & J. Schacter (Eds.), *Linguistic Perspectives on Second Language Acquisition* (pp. 183–199). Cambridge: Cambridge University Press.

Gass, S. M., & Madden, C. G. (Eds.). (1985). *Input in second language acquisition.* Rowley, MA: Newbury House.

Gass, S. M., & Schachter, J. (Eds.). (1989). *Linguistic perspectives on second language acquisition.* Cambridge: Cambridge University Press.

Gass, S. M., & Selinker, L. (Eds.). (1983). *Language transfer in language learning.* Rowley, MA: Newbury House.

Gass, S. M., & Selinker, L. (Eds.). (1992). *Language transfer in language learning.* Amsterdam: Benjamins.

Gass, S. M., & Selinker, L. (Eds.). *Second language acquisition: An introductory course.* Hillsdale, NJ: Erlbaum.

Glass, W. R. (1994). Paper delivered at the annual meeting of the American Association for Applied Linguistics, Baltimore.

Glisan, E. (1985). The effect of word order on listening comprehension and pattern retention: An experiment in Spanish as a foreign language. *Language Learning, 35,* 443–472.

Guntermann, G. (1992). An analysis of interlanguage development over time: Part II, *Ser* and *estar. Hispania, 75,* 294–303.

Harley, B., & Swain, M. (1984). The interlanguage of immersion students and its implications for second language teaching. In A. Davies, C. Criper, & A. P. R. Howatt (Eds.), *Interlanguage* (pp. 291–311). Edinburgh: Edinburgh University Press.

Hatch, E. (1983). Simplified input and second language acquisition. In R. W. Andersen (Ed.), *Pidiginization and Creolization as Language Acquisition* (pp. 64–88). Rowley, MA: Newbury House.

Hulk, A. (1991). Parameter setting and the acquisition of word order in L2 French. *Second Language Research, 7,* 1–34.

Hyltenstam, K. (1987). Markedness, language universals, language typology, and second language acquisition. In C. W. Pfaff (Ed.), *First and second language acquisition processes* (pp. 55–78). Cambridge, MA: Newbury House.

Issidorides, D. C., & Hulstijn, J. H. (1992). Comprehension of grammatically modified and nonmodified sentences by second language learners. *Applied Psycholinguistics, 13,* 147–171.

Just, M. A., & Carpenter, P. A. (1993). A capacity theory of comprehension: Individual differences in working memory. *Psychological Review, 99,* 122–149.

Klein, W. (1986). The problem of analysis. *Second language acquisition.* Cambridge: Cambridge University Press.

Krashen, S. (1982). *Second language acquisition and second language learning.* London: Longman.

Krashen, S. D. (1985). *The input hypothesis*. London: Longman.

Krashen, S. D., & Terrell, T. D. (1983). *The natural approach: Language acquisition in the classroom*. San Francisco: Alemany Press.

Lachman, R., Lachman, J., & Butterfield, E. (1979). Consciousness and attention. *Cognitive psychology and information processing: An introduction*. Hillsdale, NJ: Erlbaum.

Larsen-Freeman, D. (1976). An explanation for the morpheme acquisition order of second language learners. *Language Learning, 26,* 125–134.

Larsen-Freeman, D. (1986). *Techniques and principles in language teaching*. Oxford: Oxford University Press.

Larsen-Freeman, D., & Long, M. H. (1991). *An introduction to second language acquisition research*. London: Longman.

Lee, J. F., & VanPatten, B. (1995). *Making communicative language teaching happen*. New York: McGraw-Hill.

Lee, J. F. (1987). Morphological factors influencing pronominal reference assignment by learners of Spanish; Dedicated to Joseph H. Matluck. In T. A. Morgan, J. F. Lee, & B. VanPatten (Eds.), *Language and language use: Studies in Spanish* (221–232). Lanham, MD: University Press of America.

Leow, R. (1993). To simplify or not to simplify: A look at intake. *Studies in Second Language Acquisition, 15,* 333–355.

Lightbown, P., & Spada, N. (1993). *How languages are learned*. Oxford: Oxford University Press.

Lightfoot, D. (1993). Why UG needs a learning theory: triggering verb movement. In C. Jones (Ed.), *Historical linguistics: Problems and perspectives* (pp. 190–214). London: Longman.

LoCoco, V. (1987). Learner comprehension of oral and written sentences in German and Spanish: The importance of word order. In B. VanPatten, T. Dvorak, & J. F. Lee (Eds.), *Foreign language learning: A research perspective* (pp. 119–129). Cambridge, MA: Newbury House.

Long, M. H. (1983). Native speaker/non-native speaker conversation and the negotiation of comprehensible input. *Applied Linguistics, 4,* 126–141.

Long, M. H. (1991). Focus on form: a design feature in language teaching methodology. In K. de Bot, D. Coste, R. Ginsberg, & C. Kramsch (Eds.), *Foreign language research in cross cultural perspective* (pp. 39–52). Amsterdam: John Benjamins.

MacWhinney, B., & Bates. E. (Eds.). (1989). *The cross-linguistic study of sentence processing*. Cambridge: Cambridge University Press.

Mangubhai, F. (1991). The processing behaviors of adult second language learners and their relationship to second language proficiency. *Applied Linguistics, 12,* 268–297.

Marcel, A. J. (1983). Conscious and unconscious perception: Experiments on visual masking and word recognition. *Cognitive Psychology, 15,* 197–237.

McDonald, J. (1989). The acquisition of cue-category mappings. In B. MacWhinney & E. Bates (Eds.), *The cross-linguistic study of sentence processing* (pp. 375–396). Cambridge: Cambridge University Press.

McDonald, J. L., & Heilenman, L. K. (1992). Changes in sentence processing as second language proficiency increases. In R. J. Harris (Ed.), *Cognitive processing in bilinguals* (pp. 325–336). Elsevier.

McDonald, J., & MacWhinney, B. (1989). Maximum likelihood models for sentence processing. In B. MacWhinney & E. Bates (Eds.), *The cross-linguistic study of sentence processing* (pp. 397–421). Cambridge: Cambridge University Press.

McLaughlin, B. (1987). *Theories of second language acquisition.* London: Edward Arnold.

McLaughlin, B. (1990). "Conscious" versus "unconscious" learning. *TESOL Quarterly, 24,* 617–634.

Musumeci, D. (1989). *The ability of second language learners to assign tense at the sentence level: A cross-linguistic study.* Unpublished doctoral thesis, University of Illinois at Urbana-Champaign.

Nam, E. (1975). Child and adult perceptual strategies in second language acquisition. Paper presented at the 1975 TESOL Convention, Los Angeles.

Nunan, D. (1989). *Designing Tasks for the Communicative Classroom.* Cambridge: Cambridge University Press.

Odlin, T. (Ed.). (1994). *Perspectives on Pedagogical Grammar.* Cambridge: Cambridge University Press.

Paulston, C. B. (1972). Structural pattern drills. In H. B. Allen & R. N. Campbell (Eds.), *Teaching English as a second language* (pp. 129–138). New York: McGraw-Hill.

Peters, A. (1983). *The units of language acquisition.* Cambridge: Cambridge University Press.

Peters, A. M. (1985). Language segmentation: Operating principles for the perception and analysis of language. In D. I. Slobin (Ed.), *The cross-linguistic study of language acquisition, vol. 2: Theoretical issues* (pp. 1029–1067). Hillsdale, NJ: Erlbaum.

Pica, T. (1985). Linguistic simplicity and learnability: Implications for syllabus design. In K. Hyltenstam & M. Piennemann (Eds.), *Modeling and assessing second language acquisition* (pp. 137–152. Clevedon, UK: Multilingual Matters.

Pienemann, M. (1987). Psychological constraints on the teachability of languages. In C. Pfaff (Ed.), *First and second language acquisition processes* (pp. 143–168). Cambridge, MA: Newbury House.

Pléh, C. (1989). The development of sentence interpretation in Hungarian. In B. MacWhinney & E. Bates (Eds.), *The cross-linguistic study of sentence processing* (pp. 158–184). Cambridge: Cambridge University Press.

Pollock, J. Y. (1989). Verb movement, universal grammar, and the structure of IP. *Linguistic Inquiry, 20,* 365–424.

Posner, M. I., & Petersen, S. E. (1990). The attention system of the human brain. *Annual Review of Neuroscience, 13,* 25–42.

Posner, M. I., & Rothbart, M. K. (1992). Attentional mechanisms and conscious experience. In A. D. Milner & M. D. Rugg (Eds.), *Foundations of Neuropsychology Series* (pp. 91–112). New York: Academic Press.

Posner, M., & Snyder, C. (1975). Attention and cognitive control. In R. Solso (Ed.), *Information processing and cognition: The Loyola symposium* (pp. 55–85). Hillsdale, NJ: Erlbaum.

Radford, A. (1990). *Syntactic theory and the acquisition of English syntax: The nature of early child grammars of English.* Oxford: Blackwell.

Reber, A. S. (1976). Implicit learning of synthetic languages: the role of instructional set. *Journal of Experimental Psychology: Human Learning and Memory, 2,* 88–94.

Richards, J. C., & Rodgers, T. S. (1986). *Approaches and methods in language teaching: A description and analysis.* Cambridge: Cambridge University Press.

Rutherford, W. (1987.) *Second language grammar: Learning and teaching.* London: Longman.

Rutherford, W., & Sharwood Smith, M. (1988). Consciousness raising and universal grammar. In W. Rutherford & M. Sharwood Smith (Eds.), *Grammar and second language teaching* (pp. 107–116). New York: Newbury House.

Sanz-Alcalá, C. (1994). *Task, mode and the effects of input-based explicit instruction.* Unpublished doctoral thesis, The University of Illinois at Urbana-Champaign.

Savignon (1983). *Communicative competence: Theory and classroom practice.* Reading, MA: Addison-Wesley.

Schmidt, R. (1990). The role of consciousness in second language learning. *Applied Linguistics, 11,* 129–158.

Schmidt, R. (1994). Deconstructing consciousness in search of useful definitions for applied linguistics. *AILA Review, 11,* 11–26.

Schwartz, B. (1993). On explicit and negative data effecting and affecting competence and linguistic behavior. *Studies in Second Language Acquisition, 15,* 147–163.

Selinker, L. (1972.) Interlanguage. *International Review of Applied Linguistics, 10,* 209–231.

Sharwood-Smith, M. (1985). From input to intake: On argumentation in second language acquisition. In S. M. Gass & C. G. Madden (Eds.), *Input in second language acquisition* (394–403). Rowley, MA: Newbury House.

Sharwood Smith, M. (1986). Comprehension versus acquisition: two ways of processing input. *Applied Linguistics, 7,* 239–274.

Sharwood Smith, M. (1991). Speaking to many minds: On the relevance of different types of language information for the L2 learner. *Second Language Research, 7,* 118–132.

Sharwood Smith, M. (1993.) Input enhancement in instructed SLA: Theoretical bases. *Studies in Second Language Acquisition, 15,* 165–180.

Slobin, D. I. (1966). Grammatical transformations and sentence comprehension in childhood and adulthood. *Journal of Verbal Learning & Verbal Behavior, 5,* 219–227.

Slobin, D. (1973). Cognitive prerequisites for the development of grammar. In C. Ferguson & D. Slobin (Eds.), *Studies of child language development* (pp. 175–208). New York: Holt, Rinehart, & Winston.

Slobin, D. (1985). Cross-linguistic evidence for the language-making capacity. In D. Slobin (Ed.), *The cross-linguistic study of language acquisition, vol. 2: Theoretical issues* (pp. 1157–1249). Hillsdale, NJ: Lawrence Erlbaum Associates.

Slobin, D., & Bever, T. G. (1982). Children use canonical sentence schemas: A cross-linguistic study of word order and inflections. *Cognition, 12,* 229–265.

Spada, N., & Lightbown, P. (1993). Instruction and the development of questions in L2 classrooms. *Studies in Second Language Acquisition, 15,* 205–224.

Swain, M. (1985). Communicative competence: Some roles of comprehensible input and comprehensible output in its development. In S. M. Gass & C. G. Madden (Eds.), *Input in second language acquisition* (235–253). Rowley, MA: Newbury House.

Swain, M., & Lapkin, S. (1989). Canadian immersion and adult second language teaching: What's the connection? *Modern Language Journal, 75,* 150–159.

Terrell, T. D. (1991). The role of grammar instruction in a communicative approach. *Modern Language Journal, 75,* 52–63.

Todd, L. (1974.) *Pidgins and Creoles.* Boston: Routledge.

Tomlin, R., & Villa, V. (1994). Attention in cognitive science and second language acquisition. *Studies in Second Language Acquisition, 16,* 183–204.

Towell, R., & Hawkins, D. (1994). *Approaches to second language acquisition.* Clevedon, UK: Multilingual Matters.

Trahey, M., & White, L. (1993). Positive evidence and preemption in the second language classroom. *Studies in Second Language Acquisition, 15,* 181–204.

van Naerssen, M. (1981). Generalizing secong language hypotheses across languages: A test case in Spanish as a second language. Unpublished Ph.D. thesis, the University of Southern California.

VanPatten, B. (1984a). Processing strategies and morpheme acquisition. In F. R. Eckman, L. H. Bell, & D. Nelson (Eds.), *Universals of second language acquisition* (pp. 88–98). Rowley, MA: Newbury House.

VanPatten, B. (1984b). Learners' comprehension of clitic pronouns: More evidence for a word order strategy. *Hispanic Linguistics, 1,* 57–67.

VanPatten, B. (1985a). The acquisition of ser and estar by adult learners of Spanish: A preliminary investigation of transitional stages of competence. *Hispania, 68,* 399–406.

VanPatten, B. (1985b). Communicative value and information processing in second language acquisition. In E. Judd, P. Nelson, & D. Messerschmittz (Eds.), *On TESOL '84: A brave new world.* Washington, DC: TESOL, 88–99.

VanPatten, B. (1987a). Classroom learner's acquisition of ser and estar: Accounting for developmental patterns. In B. VanPatten, T. Dvorak, & J. F. Lee (Eds.), *Foreign language learning: A research perspective* (pp. 61–75). Cambridge, MA: Newbury House.

VanPatten, B. (1987b). Classroom and naturalistic language acquisition: A comparison of two case studies in the acquisition of clitic pronouns in Spanish; Dedicated to Joseph H. Matluck. In T. A. Morgan, J. F. Lee, & B. VanPatten (Eds.), *Language and language use: Studies in Spanish* (pp. 241–262). Lanham, MD: University Press of America.

VanPatten, B. (1988). How juries get hung: problems with the evidence for a focus on form in teaching. *Language Learning, 38,* 243–260.

VanPatten, B. (1990). Attending to content and form in the input: An experiment in consciousness. *Studies in Second Language Acquisition, 12,* 287–301.

VanPatten, B. (1991). Grammar instruction and input processing. Paper presented at the special colloquium on the Role of Grammar Instruction in Communicative Language Teaching, Concordia University and McGill University, Montreal.

VanPatten, B. (1993). Grammar teaching for the acquisition-rich classroom. *Foreign Language Annals, 26,* 435–450.

VanPatten, B. (1994). Evaluating the role of consciousness in second language acquisition: Terms, linguistic features and research methodology. *AILA Review, 11,* 27–36.

VanPatten, B. (1995). Cognitive aspects of input processing in second language acquisition. In P. Heshemipour, I. Maldonado, & M. van Naerssen (Eds.), *Festschrift for Tracy David Terrell* (pp. 170–183). New York: McGraw-Hill.

VanPatten, B., & Cadierno, T. (1993). Explicit instruction and input processing. *Studies in Second Language Acquisition, 15,* 225–243.

VanPatten, B., Lee, J. F.,& Ballman, T. L. (1996). *¿Sabias que...?* (2nd ed.). New York: McGraw Hill.

VanPatten, B., Lee, J. F., Glass, W. R., & Binkowski, D. D. (1992). *Manual to Accompany ¿Sabias que...?* New York: McGraw Hill.

VanPatten, B., & Oikkenon, S. (1996). The causative variables in processing instruction: Explanation vs. structured input activities. *Studies in Second Language Acquisition.*

VanPatten, B., & Sanz, C. (1995). From Input to Output: Processing Instruction and Communicative Tasks. In F. Eckman, D. Highland, P. W. Lee, J. Mileham, R R. Weber (Eds.), *Second Language Acquisition and Pedagogy* (pages unavailable). Hillsdale, NJ: Erlbaum.

White, L. (1987). Against comprehensible input: The input hypothesis and the development of second-language competence. *Applied Linguistics, 8,* 95–110.

White, L. (1989). *Universal grammar and second language acquisition.* Amsterdam: Benjamins.

White, L. (1991). Adverb placement in second language acquisition: Some effects of positive and negative evidence in the classroom. *Second Language Research, 7,* 133–161.

White, L. (1992). Long and short verb movement in second language acquisition. *Canadian Journal of Linguistics, 37,* 273–286.

White, L., Spada, N., Lightbown, P., & Ranta, L. (1991). Input enhancement and L2 question formation. *Applied Linguistics, 12,* 416–432.

Whittlesea, B. W. A., & Dorken, M. D. (1993). Incidentally, things in general are particularly determined: An episode-processing account of implicit learning. *Journal of Experimental Psychology: General, 12,* 227–248.

Wickens, C. D. (1984). Processing resources in attention. In R. Parasurman & D. R. Davies (Eds.), *Varieties of attention.* New York: Academic Press.

Winitz, H. (Ed.). (1981). *The comprehension approach to foreign language acquisition.* Rowley, MA: Newbury House.

Wolfe Quintero, K. (1992). Learnability and the acquisition of extraction in relative clauses and wh- questions. *Studies in Second Language Acquisition, 14,* 39–71.

Wong-Fillmore, L. (1976). *The second time around.* Unpublished Ph. D. thesis, UC Berkeley.

Zobl, H. (m. s.). Lexical-functional modularity in the lexicon and the interface debate in L2 pedagogy. Unpublished manuscript.

Zobl, H. (m.s.). Critical reflections on the weak interface hypothesis. Carleton University, Canada.

AUTHOR INDEX

SUBJECT INDEX